GENERATION
WHAT

GENERATION WHAT

Dispatches From
The Quarter-Life Crisis

EDITED BY BESS VANRENEN

speck press
denver

Published by: *speck press*, speckpress.com

Printed and bound in Canada
Printed using 100% post-consumer waste recycled paper
speck press is a member of the **Green Press Initiative**
ISBN: 1-933108-12-6, ISBN13: 978-1-933108-12-4
Book layout and design by: **CORVUS**, corvusdesignstudio.com

Library of Congress Cataloging-in-Publication Data

Generation what? : dispatches from the quarter-life crisis / [edited by]
Bess Vanrenen,
p. cm.
ISBN-13: 978-1-933108-12-4 (pbk. : alk. paper)
ISBN-10: 1-933108-12-6 (pbk. : alk. paper)
1. Young adults--Attitudes. 2. Young adults--Psychology. 3. Young
adults--Biography. 4. Generation Y--Attitudes. 5. Generation Y--
Psychology. 6. Adulthood--Psychological aspects. I. Vanrenen, Bess.

HQ799.5.G457 2007

10 9 8 7 6 5 4 3 2 1

To Jared, for lots and lots of reasons; to my parents, for being smart, interesting, and wonderful people.

＊

ACKNOWLEDGMENTS Thanks to the contributors for sharing their stories, some, amazingly, before I had anything to offer them in return. Thanks to Derek Lawrence for his interest in this project, to Amy Haimerl, Jared Jacang Maher, and my family for their help editing, to Susan Hill Newton for her *enormous* help strengthening the writing throughout, and to Margaret McCullough for the fabulous cover and interior design.

TABLE OF CONTENTS

INTRODUCTION

A new generation is storming college campuses and big cities, vying for entry-level positions, buying sensible but chic cars, and sporting outfits that will later give reason to blush. They go by any number of names: Gen Y, *The Simpson*'s Generation, the Pepsi Generation, the MTV Generation... Quick, define them! Read *Salon* or *Slate*, watch MTV or just the local news, they all have a word on the subject—even the commercials.

"Gen Yers are multitaskers. Their time is important to them. They work so they can play," explains a stern, but affable, blonde anchorwoman, while doing a piece on youths in the workplace. "This generation is lazy. They have no accountability," an aging baby boomer complains about the company's younger employees. "They're young, bright, brazen!" counters another. "They need to quit whining and get a job," chimes in one more voice.

Cultural critics can't even agree on the age group under discussion. Here's one list of designations used by some advertisers: Matures, born 1909–1945; Baby

Boomers, born 1946–1964; Generation X, born 1965–1984; Generation Y or Milleniums, born 1985–present. However, Rob Owens, author of *Gen X TV*, includes just those born between 1965 and 1975.

On one subject, though, many agree. It appears as though twentysomethings and, yes, even thirtysomethings today have a hard time figuring out what to do with their (our) lives, and this apparent indecision triggers strong reactions. Some young people undoubtedly relate, while others think it's a hot crock of crap. This set of parents welcomes their child back to the hearth, but that pair kicks the kid to the curb. Many in this age group seem to be suffering from what's now called a quarter-life crisis, and here we have the subject of *Generation What?*

Alexandra Robbins and Abby Wilner, who co-wrote *Quarterlife Crisis* in 2001, noticed how so many twentysomethings felt lost on the road from young adulthood to adulthood. In their book, they identified six major signs of such a crisis: You do not know what you want; your twenties are not what you expected; you have a fear of failure; you cannot let go of childhood; you waffle over decisions; and you constantly compare.

They brought the term into the pop-culture realm, and it caught on like an STD. Musicians such as John Mayer as well as sociologists have accepted it into their lexicon. The references to the feelings associated with a quarter-life crisis are rampant in movies, TV shows, songs, and blogs. The romantic comedy *Quarter Life Crisis* came out in 2006 as well as a novel called *Twentysomething: The Quarter-Life Crisis of Jack Lancaster*, and there's an L.A. band going by the same moniker. Even Ph.D.s are studying how the period between adolescence and adulthood has widened to unforeseen proportions. Some of these books include *On the Frontier of Adulthood, Emerging Adulthood: The Winding Road from the Late Teens Through the Twenties,* and *The Changing Adolescent Experience: Societal Trends and the Transition to Adulthood.*

So what's the difference between a quarter-life crisis and a mid-life crisis, or any other life crisis for that matter? Haven't twenty year olds been having breakdowns since ...forever?

The twenties are a particularly volatile age. Look, for instance, at the poets of the nineteenth and twentieth centuries. Suicide, institutionalization, suicide again, breakdowns, manic episodes (that typically involved posturing around London in a cape) all come to mind. The Lost Generation, the Greatest Generation, and the Beat Generation were all filled with tortured souls.

But different social circumstances—whether it's a world war, an economic depression, or even a boom— bring on changes to the existing social norms and the way humans relate to each other. As a result, the crisis a young person experiences today may be distinct from ones felt in years past.

Back in the fifties and early sixties, most young Americans were getting married and having babies by their early twenties. Folks found a job after high school or college and stuck with it to the bitter end. Sex before marriage was the exception, not the rule (at least that's what they say). But the civil rights movement, the sexual revolution, feminism, and anti-war protests of that era changed the future for kids.

Picture a hip lady of Dylan's times-they-are-a-changing era. Long hair flowing, she attends a few protests at her college campus. At some point, she meets a like-minded fellow and they run off to the courthouse to get married. Though she has a lot more freedom than her mother, there are still a lot of careers she can't really pursue, a lot of lifestyles not quite available to her. Soon she has a baby in tow, and since she is getting paid much less than her hubby anyway, she decides to quit working and take care of the child. She will undoubtedly raise this child much differently than her parents' raised her. Now, picture her grown-up daughter.

Older generations paved the way for a whole new style of living. Rather than feeling compelled to settle down at twenty-one, the new generation can go to college or opt out, date several people, try out a few different jobs, and wait until they're ready for marriage. They don't have to get married either, or if they're gay they can't, but that's a whole different story.

Social revolutions aside, the opulence of the post-World-War-II era, subsequent economic booms, industrialization, and post-industrialization also all contributed to the way of life today. Suddenly, many parents in the West, especially in the United States, could afford to financially support their children after the typical period of growth and maturation had passed. Many more moms and dads could pay for college education for their kids.

One of the most fascinating things to come out of this new phase in life is that it is no longer a "phase." It can be a whole era, spanning several years. Decades ago, the groundbreaking sociologist Erik Erikson coined the term "prolonged adolescence" to describe the years between adolescence and adulthood in industrial societies. He writes that adults give young people "psychosocial moratorium" to experiment with different roles before committing to an adult identity. This is truer than ever today.

But, wait, there's a problem, and here is where the quarter-life crisis creeps in. Twentysomethings today aren't exactly reveling in their lack of restrictions, social, economic, or otherwise. In a way, it appears like there is too much freedom these days, too many choices. And these societal changes don't just hit the middle to upper classes, this is a widespread movement: What school to go to? What subject to study? Who to date? Who to marry? What career to pursue? Seem like nice problems to have, right? But for anyone who's been sold the American dream, it's actually quite overwhelming.

Not only are young people surrounded by hundreds of new options, there is also a disparity between what they see and what they can grab hold of. Once high school graduates think they have made a decision, they just might realize that what they want and what they can get are two *very* different things. This is important to realize. The quarter-life crisis is not just a crisis of indecision; it is also a crisis of closed doors. The American dream says any child can grow up to be President of the United States. In high school and college, kids believe this is more or less true. It is somewhat beautiful—the hope that is felt at that age—but it also leads almost directly to disillusionment. Not everyone can become the president or a major league baseball player. Not everyone can go to Harvard Law School. Not everyone can write for *The New Yorker*. Some of what leads to success is natural ability, some of it is confidence and perseverance, and—for better or for worse—some of it is connections and even luck. Plus, no matter what those people against affirmative action say, it is just not that easy (for a whole slew of reasons) for a Hispanic girl from a poor urban area to find her way to med school. This is *not* to say young adults should not dream. But they should be aware of what is stacked against them so if they have the will to, they can surmount it.

It also seems like there is a lot of pressure on young people these days to accomplish great and huge things: write a novel or a screenplay; become a movie star; finish med school; move from editorial assistant to assistant editor to editor in record time; and make gargantuan salaries. Pop culture's obsession with youth adds to that pressure. Unfortunately, the twenty-three-year-old novelist is much more marketable than the forty-one-year-old one, just as a twenty-six-year-old lawyer is often seen as "worth" more than an older attorney. The pervasive images seen in magazines and on the Internet and television of twentysomethings and thirtysomethings clad in designer jeans, lounging around at coffee shops and in cool cars, don't help either. So, the quarter-life crisis hits about the time when prolonged instability finally becomes anxiety, and the sense that anything is possible just doesn't coalesce with the facts of the "real world."

Common sense says that there are, more or less, two types of quarter-life crises. There is the young adult who gets a job right out of high school or college, but then begins to question if that job is really a good fit and suddenly makes a major life change. And there is the one who does not necessarily finish school (at least not in a hurry), cannot really figure out what to do, and flounders around for awhile not committing to anything. Usually the latter comes to hate the instability of that kind of life and eventually settles down in some way, even clinging desperately to something stable, like a job or a partner.

Yet, a refusal to commit immediately to adulthood is not (necessarily) the result of an emotional disturbance or some other unsympathetic diagnosis. How can young folks commit when all these forces are compelling them to do otherwise? Besides in a lot of ways, it is a period of life that can be filled with exciting and wonderful experiences. During this time, twentysomethings can try to figure out what in work and in love pleases them; they can dream of all different ways their life could turn out; they can worry about no one else but themselves. It is especially helpful for adolescents who come from difficult homes, who can use this time to create a life separate from that of their parents.

This project came to fruition a few years back when a writer friend had just finished an article about a man who had written some self-help book for quarter-lifers. It came up that trite advice on how to get out of the mud of the quarter-life crisis does little to help the intelligent, self-reflexive, critical, and perhaps cynical kids who get stuck on the road to adulthood. Most people know what to do; it is doing it that is the problem. Wouldn't stories from these people *in their own voices* be so much more helpful?

This book is organized by theme: finishing school, jobs, parents, and relationships. While reductive, these are indeed the topics most young folks are complaining about most of the time that they're complaining. Yes, something deeper is undoubtedly going on in the psyches of today's youth—but that's why this book gives priority to the stories over analysis or advice. Sociologists who have studied the "transition to adulthood" often use certain major events to mark this transition, namely finishing education, entering full-time work, marriage, and parenthood. These are practically the same categories laid out in this book.

I didn't put this book together to make money or a name for myself. I did it because I know first hand how hard this time can be, and since it's a relatively new phenomenon there are not necessarily a lot of resources out there for support. I wanted to provide a cohesive, interesting, insightful book. *Generation What?* is a book for those filled with the anxiety and despair that this time in life often brings. Again, this book is not everything to all people. Hopefully, if you are in the midst of a mid-twenties/thirties crisis, you will find a story in here that echoes your own. If not, you can at least laugh and cry with the writers as they expose their stories. And

I encourage you to write, draw, paint, *whatever*, your own quarter-life crisis story. I had a really hard time writing my own because I had to relive, essentially, the painful experiences I had at twenty-four. Many of the contributors said the exact same thing. But I promise, there is relief just in getting it out, and there is something else—something somewhat intangible—in sharing it with other people. So to those, especially, who are part of Generation What, enjoy.

part:

1

ALMA

MUTTER

We don't need a college—or even a high school—degree to have a successful life, but it seems to help. We also don't need a degree to have a quarter-life crisis, but it too seems to help.

For those of us who make it to campus, it can be the most memorable and rewarding experience. Some of us discover who we are, enjoy a few carefree years without parents or nagging responsibilities (except for those pesky exams), and learn things we probably never could have otherwise. Others of us are more motivated, excited to march right out and change the world, armed only with degrees in fist.

Higher education has its downside, as well—the depression caused by feelings of displacement and homesickness, the anxiety over the constant competition. College kids also complain about the futility of, namely, a liberal arts education ("When am I going to need to know about 'The Wife of Bath's Tale' in the real world?"), especially when a ten-page paper on Chaucer is due at 8 a.m. the following morning.

When we have to cough up the cost of college tuition, and when all those darned bills (that we can't really cover without the income from a full-time job) start adding up, that's when undergrads really start questioning the real-world payoff of that Chaucer paper. A lot of students—more and more every year, it seems—are having to take out daunting loans to pay for school, and for that college-kid lifestyle. But somehow the bills have to get paid, and with tuition on the rise it's only getting more difficult. Is it any wonder questions arise as to whether said degree is actually "worth" it?

Then, of course, there's commencement. Graduating from high school and college is strangely both numbingly mundane and earth shaking; just like the morning of a birthday when twenty-five feels exactly like twenty-four. How exactly are we any different? But maybe new doors will open up, and that perfect life really does lie just around the corner. Or, maybe not.

DARKER COUNTRY

by *Hal Niedzviecki*

I'm in the computer lab. It's late afternoon, late fall. Outside it's already getting dark. It gets dark early here, in the computer lab, in Edinburgh, a city in Scotland that, though warmer than the Canadian city I came from, seems so dark and cold, a winter place.

I am twenty-three years old. The room is a quarter occupied. Heads arch toward screens. The rows of computers buzz, a collective hive of purposeful energy...the clacking of keys. What is the purpose? It is before cell phones, email, laptops in every lap. I am writing an essay. Joyce. Beckett. Woolf. Those dour, optimistic modernists. I am hungover. Hunched into the screen, I type furiously. I drink every night. I will drink tonight. I type angrily. I believe in written words, but am always angry at them— the way a teenager believes in, and hates, his father. I am trying to say something about these writers. I am trying to impress a certain professor who wrote his dissertation on Bob Dylan and seems like someone I might become, despite his earring and his studied mannerisms.

All this in my mind, and other things. A girl in Israel. A song lyric stuck in my head, a crooned line sounding more meaningful than it really is. Beckett. Malloy, Mallone. Breaking the waves, Woolf's polite alter egos attend an interminable garden party. Bloom's bacon breath.

It happens like this: a darkness splitting a darkness. A hole opens and I fall in. It only takes a few seconds. I look up, look around. Did anyone else notice the rupture appearing in the small space between the computer screen and my head? Did anyone else see that I had fallen in, pulled myself out with a desperate frantic jerk? No one noticed. Pale students typing, keeping to themselves. I am sweating. I am acutely aware of my breathing. I lurch backwards, stand. The room spins. I close my eyes. The dark kaleidoscopes. The floor pitches. I feel my legs under me, week, wobbly, swaying. I open my eyes, grab my knapsack, and stagger out of the computer lab.

*

I walk with my arms in front of me, zombie style. I am afraid of falling, of running into things that should be stationary but are now in motion.

My residence room is a forty-minute walk from campus. It's a walk I am slowly getting used to.

I lumber through the main campus and outlying busy streets of the city before stumbling into a series of interconnected parks aptly named "The Links." The ground undulates, as if I'm part of a waking dream. Will I get used to this, too? I move with my head down. It's cold but I sweat. Sweat drips off my forehead, gets lost in the grass between my feet. Everything sways. I take a quick, darting glance forward. My stomach heaves. I have seen enough: a few steps ahead of me.

The dormitory is an official university residence, but far from campus. It's in an upscale neighborhood. It houses fifty students, freshmen from Glasgow, from small Scottish towns, from mid-sized British industrial cities. A scattering of older undergrads, a bunch of sophomores doing their third year of study abroad. There are Americans, Germans, a stocky Frenchman. I am the only Canadian. We live in single and double rooms surrounded by imposing, Victorian, five-story walkups from which no one ever emerges.

My hands shaking, I pull open the big wooden door and stumble into the residence. It was a mansion once. Tall, wide staircases spill into an impressive foyer lit with a miniature chandelier. I watch my feet move up the staircase, see them carry me along a still unfamiliar threadbare carpet. I drop my keys, fumble for them in the gloom, manage to work the lock, and walk into my room. My possessions—a heap of dirty clothes, a guitar, a stack of books, a clock radio tape recorder, several bottles of whiskey and wine—haven't changed. The room is cold. It is always cold. I pull off my sweater, feel its wet wool trap my head. It comes again then, the sudden horrible yawning opening. I tear at my clothes, try to escape. I fall in.

When it's over, I am naked in the cold, white room. My window looks over the street. I am breathing very hard. I am skinny, unfit. Outside it begins to drizzle. It is nearly winter in Edinburgh. It will rain almost constantly for the next three months. I wipe the wet from my brow with a bare arm. I shiver. The small room presses around me. I take several faltering steps and fall into the narrow, single bed. I pull the rough blankets over me, curl into a fetal position, and close my eyes. It's five o'clock in the early evening. I hear the rain. I am waiting for the darkness to stop moving.

I stay in bed for several days. My only friends are the other students in the residence. We don't have a cafeteria, just small kitchens that were probably closets once, fridges divided up, cupboards stacked with cracked, stained crockery. Someone knocks on my door. I don't answer, and they leave. In the fading light of day, I stare up at the high ceiling and consider the gray-white peeling paint. When the room darkens, I don't turn the light on. I get out of bed. I feed a coin into the gas range. I sit on the wood floor in front of the fire. These ranges are the building's only heat. We get the coins from the warden, a retired lady named Elsie who lives in the basement. Each coin costs a pound, gives you heat for forty minutes.

I wake up sprawled on the floor. The fire is out. It is still night. I am out of coins. Bibi is microwaving a chicken. Bibi is also an exchange student, but he is an adult among us children, a vocal Christian with a wife and three kids back home in Nigeria. I must leave my room. The stench of cheap poultry stewing in its own radiated juices demands it.

I get dressed and go out. Just like that, I say to myself. You see? It's easy. In this city, with few friends and much time, I have taken to walking compulsively, not paying attention, aware only of a vague sense of the foreign— black scarab taxi cabs, butchers with old-fashioned signs peddling rashers and mince and haggis, pubs on every street.

I find my group in one of those pubs. Strangers to each other, we drink in a cluster, stay close to each other and the residence. Cliques and couples are slowly form- ing, but I don't belong to any of these smaller groups.

I have one person I consider a friend, my next-door neighbor, an Irishman named Liam. We have shared several sprawling pub crawls. He studies math. We drunkenly and haphazardly debate whether or not things like numbers and words can be real. Or are they always abstractions, pointless shadows obscuring the real? Will studying make us smarter or stupider? At least, that is what I think we talk about. One night, I cook Liam a lamb stew. He feeds on pub food and the occasional supermarket frozen dinner—toad-in-the-hole or steak-and-kidney pie. My lamb stew is a revelation to him. He makes me promise to teach him how to cook. I tell him that after years of boiled pork and powdered béchamel sauce, I suspect his palate is beyond redemption. You have to help me, he says. I'll give up Christianity. I'll become a Jew. He crosses himself. I swear to God, he says. We toast on it.

Liam has his own friends and does not hang out with the group. But I am here. Out of my room. The girls are plump, white, their teeth crooked. The boys scrawny, smart, self conscious, and unfashionable. I push through the crowd to the bar. I order a pint and a whiskey. I breathe in the odor of stale beer and cigarette smoke. As an odor, it isn't that different from the taste of air trapped inside the chapel of a synagogue. I visited the Edinburgh synagogue on Yom Kippur. I broke fast with a family, a middle-aged professional couple with two blonde children ages eight and ten. We sat around a nicely appointed table and spoke in a hush. It felt like nothing I was used to. There are no other Jews in the residence. I never went back to the synagogue. I don't know why I went in the first place. I promised my mother.

The pub is alive. The crowd closes around me as I wait for my drinks. This time, I feel it coming: a tightening in my shoulders, a drop in my stomach. These are the signs. The hole opening, sucking me in. I dig my fingernails into my wet palms. I close my eyes, will it to go away. Alright, mate?, asks the bartender in front of me, waiting impatiently for payment. I hand him a wet fiver, drink the whiskey while he makes change. I want to go to my room. I take the pint back to my crowd. I am safe in my room. Am I? The hole is there, too. The world lies on its side. My crowd is talking, telling stories. I stand pretending to listen, trying to listen. I drink fast, as fast as I can without attracting attention. Drink. Drink again. After several more pints, I suddenly take a turn, telling a story. We are talking about hometowns. I describe my suburban Maryland high school—cheerleaders and football players and field parties and make-out sessions in McDonald's parking lots. It's just like on TV, I say. Only weirder.

Now I am buying drinks and talking loudly. This is the cure. I am cured. Sure, why not? There is a girl—soft and round. I have bought her several drinks. Looked into her eyes while I told my stories. She laughed with the others, her lips wet with drink. We go back to my cold room. I give her whiskey. I know I must keep drinking. I know the dark hole lingers above me, not gone at all. Maybe it is gone, though. She is English. Tells me about her French boyfriend. She met him on a trip to Paris, last summer. Only months ago, but to both of us the summer is like a dream. She says he won't find out. How can he find out? I make jokes in a French accent. She giggles. I kiss her. We undress. I suggest a condom. It's okay, she says, she's on the pill. I put it in. Thrust a few times. Finish in her. I am cured, I think. It will be over now. Should I go? she asks. I don't answer. Maybe I think I am pretending to be asleep. She dresses, leaves.

I am in love with a girl in Israel. Last night I lasted only a few minutes. But when I masturbate, it can go on for hours. I am revolting and weak. Or else it isn't me at all. It is the world that is something to be endured and gotten over.

I force myself to gather my books and attend my morning class. I need to walk. I need a destination. When I arrive on campus, I cannot remember which class I am supposed to be attending. I have to pull out my binder and consult the schedule I received when I registered. I am due in a philosophy lecture, my class on Plato's dense masterpiece, *Theatetus*. The professor is an Italian, was disappointed and perplexed when he discovered on the first day of lectures that not one of us spoke a single word of Greek, ancient or otherwise. Still he persists in reading to us "from the Greek," as he announces frequently. He follows these incomprehensible readings with his own unique translation. He considers the expensive translated edition the class all bought from the university book-store vastly flawed. While he talks, I flip wildly through the pages of my thick annotated text trying to figure out which passage of Plato's he is referring to. It gives me, at least, something to do. But even when I find the right page, Plato's account of Socrates discussing the definition of knowledge with some guy named Theatetus remains slippery, a fish flashing in the sun, jumping through my soft palms. At the professor's request, I have already met with him several times to discuss my essays. I am used to getting mediocre grades—Bs, not Ds. The Greek profes-sor underlines vast swathes of my heartfelt commentary and adorns the margins with questions marks. He tells me I need to learn to make my arguments in a precise fashion according to the strictures of philosophical logic. I tell him logic makes no sense. We are at an impasse.

I feel the unbearable itch in my legs, the need to walk, move, escape. I try to ignore it. There is one little thing that puzzles me, Socrates says cutely. The professor discusses the refutation of the assertion that knowledge is perception. From the Greek, he drones. As if singled out for a question, I break into a sweat. My legs itch and my stomach drops. The hole opens. My chair abruptly tilts to one side. It does not. I hold on to keep from falling off. This is how the interminable hour passes, my eyes mostly closed, my head down, my thighs trembling and tense, my fists tight to the plastic edge of the seat.

If I cannot attend classes, I will fail. I do not want to fail. I have never been a success at anything in particular, but I have never been a failure either. My classes ground me, give me something to do. More than that: they suggest a truth. I am at a time in my life when truth seems elusive but very necessary. What is knowledge? Socrates wants to know. But I'm more interested in truth. My favorite class is "Introduction to Scottish Literature." The words read out loud by the professor fill me with an inescapable longing, a need that cannot be satisfied. Words create places, and places create words. Perhaps I can find words, create a place. What place? Already, I am asking the wrong question. I need to start from the beginning. What is knowledge? What are words? If I don't attend classes and fail, my failure will make it impossible for me to one day find the words to invent my place, not a place, really, but my own personal epistemology, answer to the age-old question Socrates never quite answers. But I am failing. I find that it is only possible to answer Socrates' question through reference, metaphor, example. This, according to my professor and Plato, is no answer at all.

Class is over. The floor shifts at random angles, causing me to stumble as I move through the hall of the philosophy building. I must look drunk. I don't drink during the day. I think that I will go to the pub and drink. I will take the cure. I will drink during the day. The cure will kill me. I will fail and die. Knowledge is what you know. Isn't it? So I force my legs to enter another building: the student clinic. I've never been here before, but walk past it often enough.

I need a doctor, I tell the lady at reception. I need to see a psychiatrist. I'm going crazy. I speak loudly, urgently. Everyone in the room stares at me. What do they see? I am skinny. My curly hair is long and greasy. My clothes are unkempt: flannel shirt and ripped jeans; it is the age of grunge—Nirvana, Pearl Jam, Soundgarden. I am accidentally in style.

You have to see a regular doctor first, the receptionist coldly informs me. I take the indicated seat. I sit digging my fingernails into the soft part of my hands. I endure side-long glances. They probably think I'm an American.

The regular doctor is a young Irishman. He reminds me of my Dylan-loving modernist professor. I think I will relate to him. I will make a joke and he will realize that underneath that joke is someone desperate and scared. He will help me.

I'm going crazy, I tell the doctor. I bet you don't hear that everyday. He looks at me impassively, unconcerned, not amused. Yes, well, he says noncommittally.

I tell him about the dizziness, claustrophobia, agoraphobia, inability to sit still, moments that come out of nowhere and swallow me up. I tell him that after these dark ripping moments, I am shaky and weak and unable to focus on anything but putting my feet in front of me, one after the other, walking for hours with my head down. I am having these moments three or four times a day.

Panic attacks, the doctor tells me. They are very common in young students. I see them all the time. His Irish brogue is friendly but his tone is curt and annoyed. He sees them all the time. I wait for him to cure me.

Just don't think about it and they'll go away, he says. Okay, son?

I look down at my boots. They are scuffed, filthy with mud from the wet Links.

The doctor writes something in a file. He puts a hand on my shoulder and steers me out of the examination room.

Good luck, he says with finality.

•

I don't go to my classes or the pub. I spend my days walking. The air is cool, the city reserved, cold, posh. Princess Street, the castle, Arthur's Seat looming around a wrong turn. At night I take the cure. Drunk, the hole disappears. I am loud, confident, my long, curly, greasy hair hiding my face.

I drink with the group, with Liam, in the television common room, alone in my room, sitting on the floor with Beckett's trilogy on my lap, the words barely illuminated by the light of the gas fire.

One night, Liam and I decide we will have a pint at every pub we pass as we walk toward the center of the city. It's a daunting task. Pubs close at midnight. It's already seven. If we are to make it even halfway, we'll have to drink fast. It is a Monday. At 11:30 we're eight pints and pubs in and have landed at a dark, dirty spot where a group of musicians play Gaelic folk for free drinks. The music repeats itself, swirls insistently. Liam tells me about his town in Ireland, Carrick-on-Suir in the county Tipperary. Everyone's related, he confides. I have three hundred cousins. There are two hundred pubs for five thousand people. He laughs. He is from somewhere.

I am a Jew born in a small industrial city on the edge of the Canadian side of a great lake. We moved from that city when I was a month old. I got pneumonia during the move, spent my second month of life in the hospital. My parents were born in Poland, lived through World War II in the USSR, a country their parents had the sense to flee as soon as the war was over. Now they live in the suburbs of Washington, D.C. I am in Edinburgh, piss-drunk with an Irishman. My girl is in Israel. I met her in Toronto, where I am attending university. I let her go. I shrugged and told her—we'll just breakup for the time being, see what happens when we're back. This is my side of the breakup, my comeuppance for all the years I staggered drunk into her little room on Lippincott Street, my pizza breath and dirty fingers invading her orderly solitude. I fucked her, then immediately fell asleep on her narrow mattress, my body crowding her out so that when we woke up in the morning, she was on the floor naked.

Do you ever think you might go crazy? I ask Liam suddenly.

Sure, he says. He smiles impishly. I wait for him to continue, but he drinks instead. Behind us, the fiddle plays and a lady heavy with makeup half dances, half sways.

How could you not, right? I say. I drink the remaining half of my pint in one gulp. Another? I say. Of course, Liam says.

●

I make one more attempt at going to class. I can't ride the bus, I can't brave the library stacks, I can't use an elevator, I can't see a movie or watch television, I can't remain still for longer than five minutes at a time unless I've got a drink in hand. I try to shop for groceries and find myself hyperventilating in the bright aisles of the Stainsbury's. Now I eat only when drunk, surviving on the occasional donar kebab or fish and chips with salt and sauce, whatever the group decides to snack on after the pubs close their doors.

The hole is getting bigger, encompassing more and more of my sober life. I will fall in and not be able to climb back out. That is what madness is. I don't think I am going crazy. My thoughts race, but they are my own. So what is happening to me? I imagine myself to be completely alone, suffering something incomprehensible to others. It never occurs to me that there might be books and articles on the subject, pharmaceuticals manufactured by the millions. The Irish doctor was wrong, he doesn't see what I have. Not all the time, or anytime. What I have is invisible, known only to me.

The hallway and its students spin. I suffer two small attacks wending my way to class. I keep a hand on the wall, trailing my fingers. It seems to help. I drop into a desk, perspiring profusely, knowing that I will be totally unable to listen to the lecture. My goal is just to remain. It is my favorite class. Scottish Literature. The professor is a renowned expert, a man in his fifties with an upper-class Edinburgh accent and a passion for the words of his countrymen that seems impossible to discount or diminish. Here is the real thing. Here is evidence that words, maybe only words, matter.

We read *Lilith* by George MacDonald. *Peter Pan* by J.M. Barrie. We read James Kelman and Alasdair Gray. All are imaginers of dreamscape Scotland. They envision a country that is not a country, which never feels quite real. We are talking about Scotland and fantasy, the region's authors a remarkable bunch of daydreamers and skywatchers. I cannot imagine fantasy. I am mired in the here and now. Later I will think: If you know where you are from, if you know who you are, you are free to imagine how the past can be the future. Without that—a history married to a landscape married to a literature—you will always write about the present in the past tense, be stuck just trying to create something tangible out of dispossession. As if on cue, the hole appears. It starts small. I blink, shake my head. It's gone. I am pale and damp. I can smell my fear. The pen is slick in my hand. I use it to jab into the palm of my hand. The pain keeps me from bolting. From falling. The hole gets bigger as the enormity of time remaining closes in on me. Three quarters of a class. My whole life. The more I think I can't make it, the more I feel the hole expanding, until it is a dark vortex floating just above my head. If I stop grinding the tip of my pen into my hand it will descend. If I stop thinking: You're okay, you're okay, you're okay, chanting a silent lying mantra, it will descend. If I look at the clock, at the professor, at the faces of my fellow students, it will descend. I close my eyes and concentrate on the spinning blackness, on the spiraling tip of the pen digging in.

Good God! I hear the professor proclaim. I open my eyes, expecting everyone to be looking at me, at the stigmata stain on my hand. But they are looking behind me. In the aisle between the desks, a girl thrashes on her back. She's having a convulsion! the professor proclaims. Students rush to her. I hurry from the room. I trip down the stairs, push open the doors with my palms. I leave a smear of blood as I burst into the wet air.

*

I am taking longer and longer showers. Normally I masturbate in the hot water, but now there seems to be something wrong with my penis. I hold it in my hand. It's shrinking. The head is white.

In the antiseptic light of the bathroom, I get as close to it as I'm able. The hole leaks just the tiniest bit of clear, viscous fluid.

These symptoms have been developing for a few weeks. I've ignored them, telling myself they would pass, saying that it's the result of chafing, the exposed tip rubbing against a pair of too-loose boxer shorts, all those hours of walking.

I'm losing weight. My face is angular, gaunt in a way it's never been before. I barely recognize myself.

I think: gonorrhea, syphilis. I think: I can't handle this. I can't fucking handle this. I dry off, go back to my room, and lock the door. I wrap myself in the coarse blankets on my bed and drink from a bottle of whiskey. I need to talk to the girl in Israel. There is one phone in the residence, a communal payphone that receives all incoming calls. In Israel, on kibbutz, there is also a single communal phone for the volunteers. She sent me the number in a letter. She said that once a week she is there, that her family calls and that I could call too at this particular time. How much would such a call cost? How does one place such a call? I have money. My parents gave me money for the year. My job is to learn, my mother is fond of saying. The girl in Israel can tell me what to do, how to do it. Even if she is disgusted with me and never wants to see me again, she will be caring and compassionate. She will listen to my problems and advise me. But then she will put down the phone and be gone. I cannot tell her about my problems. I cannot tell her that the head of my penis is cold and white. I cannot tell her that she is the only girl I last with, that with everyone else I finish in minutes, in seconds.

It is better to kill myself, I think. I do not really think I will kill myself. But maybe I will. Or should.

The Irish doctor holds my member up with a tongue depressor so he can get a good look. He doesn't seem to recall seeing me before. He asks about unprotected sex. I nod. I am day drunk, stopped in at the pub on the way.

For liquid courage. It works. I feel cocky. That's right, I want to say. Lots of it. You can pull your pants back up, he says. We both take one last look. It is pathetic, a dead inchworm barely visible in an abundant patch of tangled, sweaty pubic hair. He sends me to reception with a note—I must go to the clinic in the hospital. He doesn't comment on what may or may not be wrong with me. You'll be alright, son, he says as I leave. This time, he sounds more sincere, as if there's something actually wrong with me.

*

It's raining. I walk toward the hospital, a massive gray building surrounded by a long wall. The hospital is not far from the university. I wonder if I should tell the English girl. We still speak to each other, socialize within the group, pretend like nothing happened between us. In a way it's true. There are other girls. A lanky New Englander with blonde hair and freckles. She is also part of the group, attracts a lot of attention from the freshmen British boys who have taken to wearing scarves and berets and talking about Sartre. But she often leaves them to approach me, keeps saying I'm really funny. She's asked me to have lunch with her on campus. She is nice, pretty. I can't imagine what we would talk about during that lunch, alone over a pint at the pub, after I've stuck my shrunken worm in her and ejaculated.

At the hospital I stand by the main entrance, off to the side, getting wet in the rain. My appointment isn't until next week. The building looks dark, cavernous, maze-like. I wonder if I will be able to enter. I wait for the dark hole to appear, to suck me in. I'm getting what I deserve, I think. This is the sort of place where people like me end up. I wait, but nothing happens. I stand in front of the hospital watching the patients. Under the awning they puff away on cigarettes as attached to them as their IV drips. They seem at peace.

•

Eventually, I notice that night has fallen. It is dark. It could be 5 p.m. or 2 a.m. It gets dark early and stays dark until what seems like long after morning. My dick is a little white charcoal in my pants. Gingerly I trudge to the International Student's Center. It's just a basement lounge with a few copies of *Le Monde* and the *Herald Tribune* scattered around. I'd met some people there, a Scot whose parents live in Rome, a German girl with sandy hair and a crooked smile. Some of the regulars at the center have organized a party there tonight. Beer carted in, a sound system. It's a place to go.

I get there and things are already underway, which means it's later than I thought. I am drenched. People chatter, drink, the stereo booms. I take off my tattered trenchcoat, a thrift-store garment dragged across the ocean, as useless in the rain and wind as it was in the snow and sleet. I drop it in a dark corner. I recognize a few of the regulars. They drink Budvar from oversized bottles, a Czech beer whose namesake was borrowed to create thin, sudsy Budweiser. I tip a cold bottle to my lips and fill my mouth. The beer is rich, hoppy. Whatever happens, I think, I'll probably live. The German girl approaches me. You're all wet, she says coquettishly. No shit, I say. I buy her a beer from the makeshift bar. And another for myself. Perhaps her ancestors killed my ancestors. In Scottish literature, things that happened a thousand years ago still matter. In the language of Plato, things are proven, words are numbers, and Socrates drives the stake of logic right through the heart of the matter.

We drink as if we are very thirsty. The stereo plays "Smells Like Teen Spirit." The German girl grabs my hand and pulls me into a throng of dancers. In the near dark, the drunk crowd of foreigners jump against each other to the beat. They sing into my face. The pessimistic exuberance is infectious. I find myself thrashing my head to the beat. I feel my long hair slap my neck. Who am I? I want to transform. I am still a boy. I am waiting for things to change, to begin. The crowd of dancers mosh into each other. I am losing parts of myself. The German girl stumbles, falls into me. I catch her, feel the hot skin under her shirt. Things begin. Are beginning.

FINAL CHAPTER

by Mark Dye

My third year at college glided by even faster than the first, and now it's just hours before my senior year officially starts ticking away. The summer heat has already headed southbound, making way for the leafy, breezy fall days, then yet another too-long winter. Twenty-two years old, and I'm a goddamned elder on this stupid campus. As we head toward old age and its accompanying insignificance, when we see fewer reasons to defend our grand individuality or to espouse immoderate views, as we watch sideways in mirrors as the back crooks forward and drool flows liberally down a wrinkled crevice on the neck, this undeserving institution quite unfairly lives eternally, with its inhabitants forever youthful, radiant, and vital. Eighty years can pass and these women will still have unlined faces, east/west breast, sag-free asses, and an endearing moral deficit. So that's precisely how long I'm planning to stay. It's a new goal, beginning today. I'll not leave quietly. Kicking and screaming the whole way, I expect to be a wrinkled bag o' bones escorted to the campus property line by security guards after one-too-many bouts of snoring in class and pissing down the leg. By then, having graduated into a cranky, stoop-sitting insomniac, I'll hopefully have found ulterior meanings in the world, like building the perfect fucking birdhouse.

But it's too early to be worrying about my sixtieth year at college. For now, my humble resolution for the upcoming semester shall be a reinstatement of the small hedonisms that the art of partying (AOP) was meant to promote. A return to my roots. I believe, with some fine-tuning, AOP can still resonate with life and joy.

Supporting that notion, Will just called. He rolled into town yesterday; we're booked for a full agenda of parties to hit starting tomorrow.

Tyce is gone—just up and graduated in the spring, the fool. The guy was always a poor planner; he passed too many courses, didn't change majors enough times. I haven't seen him since early summer, since way before the road trip I took in June. He came by the house on a Friday around 9 a.m., walking right through the front door and into the bedroom on me, my summer-sweetie Windy, and our friend Patience, all semi-sleeping and sprawled in various directions across the waterbed. He paused for a moment and with a glint considered evening out the situation, then strangely wheeled and left with just a wave. He probably had meetings to attend, suits to press at the cleaners. I now realize there's a great disparity, a huge chasm between the college student and even the *recent* graduate—something radically changes even between great friends. I suppose if I ever succumb to the reigns of graduation we'll be close again and will spend the next fifty years talking about nothing but the half-memory madness that was college.

But I don't want to think about that for the moment. Because tonight I'm going to grab a bid-daddy jug of

Canadian Mist, drain a third of it with Wilt and company, and see what's what at Washington's Pub. We're going to make friends with the girls in front of the long line to get in and bust through the door like the full cavalry arriving. We'll get the DJ to play a decent song for once, and just before closing I'll find a sweet, honest lass to share it with. And the two of us will sit propped against the vibrating wall by the dance floor, eye level to the flailing-leg craziness of the club, belting the song eyes-closed like Jim Morrison—hell, I'm going to *be* the next Morrison, you fuckers just watch—and she'll describe her imperfect world to her imperfect friend, somehow in the perfect moment. We'll pool all the happiness we can scrounge between us and squander it all like idiot gamblers. And we'll stave off sad goodbyes by making the night a shade darker and stretching it just a little past dawn. Her lips shall shine in the new light. Man this night, this *year* is going be the greatest, maybe of my life.

A version of this essay first appeared in
College and the Art of Partying

11.2.04

by *Courtney E. Martin*

7 P.M., NOVEMBER 2, 2004

I am twenty-four, just out of graduate school, and feeling fine on a Tuesday evening. I decide to ride the bus, something I never do because it's too damn slow for my unhealthily ambitious mojo, but it is election night and I want to savor the moments before John Kerry's sweet victory.

As the bus slides downtown towards the party I am supposed to attend, past Barnard where I was an idealistic political science major, past H&H Bagels, past Lincoln Center, past a thousand Upper West Side yippies elbowing their way into Whole Foods for election party snacks, I think about all that I have done to secure Kerry's win, or more accurately, Bush's defeat.

I signed every single petition from Moveon.org that showed up in my inbox, regardless of how many meaningless tasks were on the ever-growing to-do list from my boss. They say Moveon is my generation's newfangled form of activism. It's hip. It's the next next. I didn't feel particularly powerful clicking enter over and over again to send a form letter to some faceless politician, but it did give me a few brief moments of self-importance. Like a morphine drip, I clicked that little button and, at least for a few seconds, experienced relief from the acute pain of feeling powerless. There was a Girl Scout smugness to my digital protest.

I joined a motley crew of urban hipsters at the Planned Parenthood one muggy evening in October to cold call unregistered women voters in Pennsylvania—one of the states rumored to be teetering between red and blue. Under normal circumstances, I despise using the phone. The connection between my fingertips and the keyboard is always far more articulate than that between my brain and my mouth. My friends leave me irritated messages, "So you're being phone phobic again, great. I guess I'll just leave you *another* frickin' message." (Translation: Grow some phone balls, wimp.)

But that phone experience was different. I got to call strangers. I got to wear a headset. I got to put on my best secretary voice. I was basically nine years old again and in my rec room, a plastic stethoscope wrapped around my head, pretending to answer very important, very adult phone calls.

During the vote-a-thon I mostly ended up talking to nice old ladies. They put the phone down to get a pen and returned twenty minutes later, breathing heavily. They asked me to repeat myself over and over again. This was no surprise. Once on a high school community service trip I had the misfortune of being chosen as the BINGO announcer at a senior citizens home. The shriveled sweet-ies spent the whole time screaming to no one in particular, "What did she say? What did that girl say?"

My biggest success of that night was when I registered a ninety-three-year-old woman who had never voted in her life. I suddenly had delusions of myself as a modern day Alice Paul, spreading the word to the widowed and infirmed that not only did they have the right to vote, but could do so by absentee ballot if their arthritis was acting up or even if they didn't want to miss their daytime TV. I was hung-up on my fair share of times, but overall it had felt promising. A shot of efficacy straight in the veins.

As the election got closer, I started exercising my political muscle closer to home. I told my boyfriend of four years that I would seriously, no *seriously*, breakup with his ass if he didn't vote. He had let the presidential election of 2000 pass by without so much as a glance in the direction of the student center where we could conveniently pull the lever. The gravitas of 2004, and perhaps my threats, had lured him to the polls. Earlier in the afternoon, I received a phone call reporting that he had not only voted, but helped an old, blind lady as well. On second thought, was that just a dramatic flare to get laid? His vote was in.

And of course, mine was, too. This morning I walked from my cramped, third-floor Brooklyn apartment to a nearby elementary school gym, swollen with hope and another feeling that I couldn't, at first, name. What was the strange strength making my spine straighter, my footfalls more resolute? Why was I smiling at strangers along the way with such knowing? As I passed a group of tiny rascals selling sugar cookies badly iced like American flags it had dawned on me...I was feeling patriotic.

As someone who grew up in suburban America, surrounded by right-wing Christian organizations and military bases, I have always identified myself in direct contrast to what I perceive as flag-waving, Jesus-corrupting hypocrisy. My post-hippie parents are more likely to fly a rainbow flag than an American one from our two-story Victorian home. We traveled to Greece and Egypt, rarely within the United States. I studied abroad in South Africa in college, living in a township with a family that honored me my first night there by killing a chicken in the backyard. I am fascinated by and proud of the world, but rarely my own country.

Here I am, at the sunrise of my adult status, feeling undeniably patriotic. I live in a country where bad things often happen—million-dollar presidential campaigns bully fear-based votes out of the electorate—but good things can happen, too. Young people across the nation can see billboards of P. Diddy in his "Vote or Die" shirt and believe that civic involvement is a necessary part of keeping it real. A veteran of unjust wars past can take a stand against unjust wars present. He can be complicated and wise and still be elected by the people. I watched the debacle that was the 2000 election, and I am sure that nothing so sketchy or disappointing can happen again.

I pulled that lever this morning with unabashed pride. It was such a brief, fleeting moment—so much less physically remarkable than politically, emotionally, even spiritually remarkable. I was inflated with possibility. I could almost hear the national anthem playing as I made my way back home, a little teary and a lot hopeful.

8 P.M.

Hope has not subsided as the bus rolls through the spectacle of Times Square. Lights are flashing everywhere, taxis honk a cacophonous chorus of impatience, tourists crane their necks to see half-naked women stretched across skyscrapers on billboards. This is America at its most commercial and sensational. We make our way past the MTV studios at a snail's pace and I look up at the giant television screen at 44th Street. ABC News is already reporting some results in the eastern states—Connecticut, Delaware, D.C., Illinois, Maryland, Massachusetts, and New Jersey are all blue. I imagine the confetti raining down on John's long, funny face.

It isn't that I am 100 percent sure that John Kerry is going to win. I am 100 percent sure of almost nothing at twenty-four—besides perhaps that my rent is overpriced and adulthood overrated. It is just that I have willed Kerry to win so passionately that I can't imagine it not working out in the end. I have an unexamined assumption that if you work hard at something...okay, if you work a little at anything, you should be rewarded.

I was raised in the ascend-and-consume eighties and the save-the-world nineties, and taught that diversity should be celebrated, styrophome banished, and college resumes packed with community service awards. As kids, my friends and I—the daughters of Madonna and the sons of Bon Jovi—were fish that swam in a sea of entitlement at a time when war was the stuff of historical novels and yellow ribbons, not a real threat. We were, generally speaking, the most wanted and spoiled children in history.

And now, we want to make history—be a part of something exciting and nation-changing and significant. We are playing "adults," nervously negotiating for promotions from assistants to executive assistants, getting entangled in complicated relationships that don't require the old rubber-band-on-the-doorknob trick (rubber band=hook-up in progress), and the truly American rite of passage in this day and age: amassing our own debt.

Acting like an adult in a participatory democracy isn't particularly glamorous, but the drama behind the election is hard to resist. My father's long-winded stories about protesting Vietnam and my mother's not-long-enough stories about seventies feminism have made me hunger for my own sea of change, my own "I was there when" story. Hollywood movies have conditioned me to want fireworks and breaking news, gorgeous and witty heroes and heroines, historical moments set to booming classical music soundtracks.

I get off the bus at Union Square and make my way over to my brother's girlfriend's apartment. They are huddled in front of her laptop—she has no television—watching the results trickle in.

"Looking good!" she shouts as she opens a bottle of beer for me. "Drink that up and then let's get some slices for the road. We got to get to Dave's apartment to celebrate with everyone."

Dave's apartment will be a living room of sprawling twentysomethings clutching potato chips, cheap beer, and one another as the map continues to be colored in the decisive hues of red and blue. Like me, Dave and his friends possess that most ridiculously expensive and sought-after of possessions: a liberal arts diploma. We have all sat through classes on Plato and his cave, Aristotle and his ethics, Machiavelli and his badittude. I, for one, swooned at Rousseau's conviction that citizens had communal responsibilities, not just rights. He seemed to believe in our best, not our worst natures. I wanted to believe in that, too.

"Oh shit," my brother, Chris, cries as a group of southern states pop up bloody red.

"What?!" I respond, looking over his shoulder at the computer screen, and then, "Oh." Oklahoma, Tennessee, the Carolinas, and Virginia are all goners.

It is moments like these when my swooning feels ridiculous. People don't vote based on political theories.

They vote based on fear, self-interest, an affinity for down-home accents. My political theory class, however inspiring at the time, is practically irrelevant in a world run by marketing and money.

Seeing my face fall, Chris goes into big-brother mode: "It's not time to freak out yet. Let's just go get some pizza and head to Dave's. Nothing significant will happen in the half hour it takes to get there." His tone reminds me of the time my parents left us at a Mexican restaurant after a long, enchilada-filled lunch. Chris, six at the time, told the hostess that we had been left behind and that he couldn't remember our phone number, but that we would be happy to drink Shirley Temples until our parents realized they had abandoned us. He spoke with such authority that, although I was only four and afraid of nearly everything but my mom's lap, I figured everything would be just fine.

9 P.M.

We walk into a Ray's Pizza, a little buzzed and a little scared, and order haphazardly. The television is on Fox News, not exactly a liberal kid's top choice for election updates, but the crust is thin and the cheese plentiful. More and more states are red—Nebraska, South Dakota, Texas, Wyoming. The confetti I had imagined just an hour earlier falling all over John's face is looking more like ash.

My brother, his girlfriend, and I have stopped talking. We are staring into our half-eaten slices, into our laps, at the greasy walls of the shop. My eye catches a World Trade Center poster hung crookedly with peeling scotch tape above a dead clock.

"Why do pizza shops always have posters of the World Trade Center towers?" I ask my increasingly depressed compadres. I realize it isn't the kind of question that either of them will have a bona fide answer to, but it seems worth the distraction.

After a long silence my brother mumbles, "I don't know."

His girlfriend echoes, "Me neither."

●

We slide out of the plastic booths and head to Dave's, deciding that movement will be good for our spirits. At a bodega near his apartment, we grab some beer. I have the strange compulsion to pick out orange circus peanuts, sweet tarts, pixie sticks—all candy that I have always hated.

"To be funny," I tell my brother.

He frowns, confused. "Why is shitty candy funny?" he asks.

I feel chastised, juvenile. I feel like running to my mom and screaming, "Nothing is working out how it was supposed to!" as if my birthday party has been ruined by a rambunctious boy who won't set the tea cups down nicely.

When we go through the checkout line, we are greeted with the pursed lips of a doe-eyed black woman who looks to be just a day past eighteen. Unsolicited she says, "You'll never catch me voting again."

"What?!" I ask, hoping I heard her wrong. A stranger's lament seems like the hair that will break my already stooped back.

"I'm never voting again. That shit ain't counted. I knew it already, but I just went ahead, and look what happened."

I want to open two beers, hand her one, and take a deep swig of my own. I want to convince her that the results of this election don't mean that voting is pointless.

I want to convince her, even more desperately, that we don't know the results of this election yet—that it is far too early to determine who won. She is my obstinate alter ego, manifesting in front of me. I want to change her mind so desperately because I need to change my own.

Instead I just smile knowingly, take my six-pack, and surprise myself by saying nothing more than, "I hear ya."

10 P.M.

Dave's apartment is just how I imagined it—packed with twentysomethings in various states of disrepair. His girlfriend—an accountant by day, modern dancer by night—is sitting on the floor and frowning at the television. Samantha—my brother's best friend from college—is intertwined with her boyfriend on a ratty couch. Everyone has a drink in their hands. No one looks happy.

I sit on the 1970s-era, burnt-orange exercise bike, the only available seat, and start to methodically churn in circles. The buzz from the metal wheels is soothing. No one seems to notice.

"I can't believe this is happening," says a girl I don't recognize, wearing a typical hipster uniform—Converse All-Stars, tight jeans, worn T-shirt.

"Is it actually hopeless or is there still a chance?" another chimes in.

Linda, an assistant to a wealthy Jewish man in an entertainment law firm who represents rich black men, answers dramatically, "Actually yes, yes it is hopeless."

Samantha looks at Linda and, with a big sister air, asks, "Do you need to go up on the roof and smoke a cigarette?"

"Yeah," Linda says, letting the tears in her eyes spill over.

I follow them up, thinking the fresh air might be nice. The view is beautiful, the kind of view that—on a different night—would have made me swoon with the possibility of being young and full of potential in the greatest city on earth. Tonight I can't stop looking at the lit windows that surround me from all directions, and feel horribly alienated and alone. Who lives within these little boxes of light? Are they feeling helpless, too? Why can't good people agree on a good president?

Linda is crying a drunk, unconsolable cry. Samantha is trying to console her anyway. "Four more years!?" Linda shrieks, then snorts, then takes a drag.

"Maybe it will push people to realize how bad he is. Maybe it will be what people need to get clear," Samantha suggests.

"I just don't understand," I chime in. "What is it that people see in him?"

"They're scared," Samantha wisely answers. "They're scared and they want to be taken care of. He gives them the illusion that he's the guy to do that."

I'm scared, I think, but don't say it out loud. We're all scared. We're trying to make our way in the world, scared shitless that we might not amount to anything, and now it feels like our worst fears are being confirmed—we have no power. Those ancient textbooks in Civics class that explained the voting system in archaic diagrams were, indeed, history lessons. Today, votes are bought and politicians bred. Today, a bunch of young people with the most expensively educated minds on the planet sit in cramped apartments and cry their eyes out because they see nowhere to put all of their knowledge and passion. Today, we grow grandfather cynicism before we've even become parents.

We spit out intermittent whines and declarations of disbelief, but mostly Sam, Linda, and I settle into a discomforting silence.

1 A.M.

Colorado is colored in red. Ohio is the last straw. A few of us decide to spring for a taxi we can't afford and head back to Brooklyn. It's strangely nice to be squashed in the backseat as the wind rushes through the window and tangles my day-overdue-for-a-shower hair. Even if each of us feels terribly lonely, we can't deny the proximity of our friends. Everyone slumps against one another.

As we head over the Manhattan Bridge and past an international high school that I have spent the year volunteering at, I shudder. I can't even begin to imagine what the rest of the world makes of us at this moment—an America that re-elects a guy who can't find most of their countries on the map. Apparently, Americans like to be told "because I said so"—their commander in chief as stubborn and old fashioned as their tough-love fathers back home. Unfortunately the rest of the world will be told "because I said so" with no say in the man's rise to global leadership. They will blame us—the scared, ignorant U.S. citizens.

As the taxi pulls up next to a subway station, my mind flashes forward fifteen minutes, totally alone in my bed, slightly drunk, really sad. I kiss the closest friend in the backseat a quick goodbye, throw a five-dollar bill their way, and jump out. I can take a train from here straight to my boyfriend's house. I can curl up next to him and listen to his sweet snore and it will sound just the same as it did the weekend before. Maybe it won't seem so bad.

1:30 A.M.

When I walk in he is editing some film project on deadline, the television set to the news, but humanely muted.

"Hi," I say, pausing in the doorway and looking, I'm sure, four years old and lost in the Mexican restaurant again.

"Oh, come here." he says, exactly the right thing at exactly the right time.

8 A.M., NOVEMBER 3, 2004

I wake up with a start and for one groggy minute, am not sure why my stomach feels like it is sinking through the mattress. Bad dream? Late for work? Period?

Then I look over at the remote, fallen from the bed onto the floor below, and remember. I try to inch out from under the ten-ton arm thrown across me and reach for it. Without moving a muscle, he says in a deep, gravely morning voice, "Don't do it."

"Don't do it?"

"Don't do it. When I went to bed at three, it didn't look good. It will probably look worse this morning."

I snuggle back in compliantly and realize that *everything* is worse this morning. Last night was depressing, but it included the elevating feeling of shock, the distraction of enigma. Today is just truth and coming to terms with it.

I lie in bed, unable to fall back asleep, and think about how I can adapt. *You must,* I reason. *You have to get used to the idea that you believed whole heartedly in something, that you wanted it and worked for it, but you aren't going to get it. You have to admit to your own smallness in a world that suddenly feels viciously large and unlike you.*

But even flirting with the idea of accepting this lesson—that I am far less powerful than I suspected—makes me so existentially sad. I lie on my back, noiseless tears falling down both sides of my face. I feel betrayed. I feel duped. I feel horribly naïve.

My childhood, like the childhoods of so many privileged children of the eighties and nineties, was packed with lessons about specialness. I was special. America was special. Together we were a special force in the world, blessing those less fortunate with food, medicines, MTV, and essential ideas about equality and justice. I had soaked these lessons up like a sponge, grown swollen with the belief that it was my destiny to one day become an adult who uses her special talents to help make the world a better place. (Cue Michael Jackson's "Heal the World" here.)

Sure, shit happens. Along the way I learned that adults were horribly fallible—even the good ones—and that anything that appears suspiciously perfect on the surface is usually ugly underneath: Milli Vanilli lip-synched and Bill Clinton did have relations with that girl. But none of this rocked the foundation of idealism that "Free to Be You and Me" and Oprah had so ambitiously built up.

But none of that prepared us—the generation who, as *Fight Club*'s Tyler Durden put it, "had no great cause"—for September 11th. On that day I was wedged in between a purring dorm-room radiator and my boyfriend in a tiny twin bed in uptown Manhattan, oversleeping in the fall semester of my senior year in college when the phone rang. Life as I knew it was over. Invincibility was dead. A new life began that included the presence of a humming fear. Anxiety grew in the cracks in my up-to-then unfaltering idealism. I wasn't special. I was thousands of miles away from my parents and suddenly craving a life as small and safe as possible. "I know this sounds crazy," I told my boyfriend in a whisper, "but I want to have babies."

Suddenly studying political science seemed terribly practical. We sat in class and talked about those on both extremes—the ones who said that we had it coming because of our egregious foreign policy and the ones who said that we had to take violent revenge immediately on the evil ones. I felt like I was swimming somewhere in between, my teenage righteousness seeping out of me. I drank a lot. We all drank a lot. We needed the numb.

I graduated. My parents took pictures. The everyday fear slowly subsided and in its place was a more rational, adult insecurity. *What will I do with my life? What are we doing with this country?* There was so much to wonder about, so little to do. Tiny steps towards creating a life never lived up to my expectations. My first job was a disaster. I could see that I would hold no power or responsibility for a decade at least. The only window in my first apartment bedroom faced the airshaft. I would fall asleep to the sound of the psychologist who lived downstairs doing phone sessions with depressed and broken-hearted people. I seemed to be capable of nothing but watching and waiting for my real, wonderful life to begin.

But the 2004 election presented the illusion of an opportunity. If every vote counted, than mine was imperative at a time when I mostly felt dispensable. I was regaining some of my backbone, remembering what it felt like to be convicted, outraged, in Oprah-logy, empowered. I could work towards something that I cared about and expect a fair outcome. Maybe all of that mumbo jumbo about "saving the world" that I was fed as a child wasn't totally off base. Maybe it wasn't too late to make a difference, not just in America, but for the whole holding-their-breath global family.

Re-adopting my idealistic roots was somewhat like coming back to a previously abusive boyfriend. I knew it was risky, but I had faith, and that faith felt really good. I didn't want to sit still for too long and analyze the statistics; I just wanted to ride the wave, ignoring the little voice in the back of my head that thought it was all a little dangerous, a little overzealous.

And all that led me to this: crying in a messy bed, feeling deeply alone despite being wedged underneath the body of someone I deeply love, fantasizing about a Bloody Mary. I know I have choices about how to process this whole debacle. Is it a chance to reveal just how inadequate and immoral Bush can be so that 2008 will be guaranteed? But 2008 seems an eon away. By 2008 I will be going to my friends' weddings, trying to get a mortgage, going to bed before 11 p.m. Hell, I will probably own an iron. Is this proof that I have little in common with the majority of the country, the pizza man and his son? Is this absolute and undeniable confirmation that I have no power—the grocery clerk's take?

I don't have any answers, just a strange feeling of *déjà vu*. The humming fear is back, and this time, I don't want babies. Frighteningly, I want nothing.

WELCOME TO AFGHANISTAN

by Matt Farwell

It's three in the morning and I am falling hard into a five-foot-deep ditch. Like a cartoon character, legs splaying out in front of me, I land square on my back. The wind is knocked out of my chest. Luckily my body armor and helmet absorb most of the impact, and before the last profanity can even leave my mouth the machine gunner walking fifteen meters next to me is there, pulling me up. Under the weight of sixty-five pounds of weapons, ammunition, body armor, and gear, I stumble awkwardly to my feet and continue walking towards the mountain that we have to climb to look for Taliban activity. It's not even light out yet and I'm sweating my ass off, dirty and tired, hands and legs filled with tiny thorns. This day already sucks. Welcome to Afghanistan. As Drill Sergeant Berg would say, during rainy nights at Ft. Benning, "Welcome to the motherfuckin' infantry."

Before I was climbing mountains in full battle rattle and falling in ditches, I shared a dive apartment with a capricious college roommate. Dwayne was touched, slightly. He liked to break plates and scream randomly at passersby out of our second-story window. The apartment, in a rapidly gentrifying locale but still clinging to its shady, ghetto roots, was littered with the detritus of two overeducated children of privilege—books and papers stacked on every flat surface not already occupied with beer bottles; a sink overflowing with dishes; polo shirts and khakis strewn on the floor. Life was fun but filled with a certain amount of melancholy, the material maelstrom inside the apartment acting as a window into my conflicted brain. I'd never been particularly happy in college, and by the middle of my third year things were beginning to reach a boiling point. The apartment and what went on there were just the physical manifestations of that slow boil.

My living conditions are just a little different now. Instead of an apartment shared with just one whacked-out roommate, I now have nine crazy infantrymen all crammed into one room. It is thirty feet by fourteen feet, with dusty concrete floors and furniture roughly constructed out of unfinished plywood and two-by-fours. Spread about the room is the debris of nine men in constant flux and motion—white, cold-weather boots here; dirty socks next to them; a rolled up carpet there; half-drunk bottles of water and partially eaten bags of beef jerky and ramen noodles on the shelves and scattered around the floor. Except for the four sets of body armor, helmets, and front-load equipment carriers containing 210 rounds of 5.56 mm ball ammunition; Israeli tourniquets, canteens, and night vision goggles hung neatly off each bunk; and the assortment of M4 carbines, squad automatic weapons, grenade launchers, and shotguns around each bed, it might be familiar to any of my friends in college who live in similar dumps.

"Dude, I think I want to get a tattoo on my head when I go back to the States on leave...think I'd get in trouble for that? I want like a big fucking dagger right on the top or maybe some bullet holes or maybe just cracks, you know, like my head is cracked," Clit says.

Clit and I sit in the guard tower, staring emptily at the night below, panning the horizon to look for any movement. Clit speaks each sentence like it bears the utmost importance, but at least his sentences are always interesting.

"I always had a .38 and a TEK on me. The TEK fit perfectly under the seat. I wore gloves everywhere I went. We did a lot of illegal stuff. We used to go out on overpasses with bags of shit and piss and vinegar—like that's no joke, shit and piss and vinegar—and drop it on shit." He throws his cigarette butt over the sandbag barrier on the guard tower, stands up to stretch. He's one of the best guys in the platoon, a natural soldier and leader, smart and resourceful. He's got some great stories from before he joined the Army.

*

While I was growing up, my dad was in the Air Force. When I lived in Turkey and Germany, practically all my friends were military brats. My brother served as a grunt in Ranger Battalion and the 25th Infantry Division before he became an Army helicopter pilot. As a kid the thought of being in the Army had always been in the back of my mind. When it was time to start looking at colleges, I again thought about the military, applying for ROTC scholarships to cover the cost of Duke or Yale, and considered going to West Point. To figure out if I really wanted to become a cadet, I attended a weeklong recruiting session at the U.S. Military Academy. To put it in the most delicate way possible, it sucked. The potential cadets seemed stiff, wooden, and out of touch. The actual cadets were either bitter because they were stuck at the academy on their summer break, or they just seemed too uptight to hang out with. The only one who seemed to have any sort of sense about him was a prior service infantryman who spoke with a thick West Virginia accent around the thick wad of Copenhagen that was perpetually shoved into his lower lip. Most of my days there were spent with a New Hampshire skater whose mom had tricked him into attending, bugging the hell out of the straight-laced applicants and cadets by claiming to be a socialist or refusing to get out of bed in the morning because we were: "An Army of one. A tired Army of one."

West Point was out.

Then I was rejected by my top two college choices. Not getting into Yale was crushing because my girlfriend at the time was a freshman there and I had visions of happily ever after with an Ivy League degree. Not getting into Deep Springs, a bizarre all-male cattle ranch/college hidden in the middle of the California desert and populated by twenty brilliant misfits, was somewhat less of a disappointment, simply because it seemed so far out. So I went to the University of Virginia, or "the University," because it had accepted me into its honors program and I had in-state tuition. I decided to go to college in the first place because I was scared not to, because it seemed like the only thing for a smart kid graduating from an exclusive private boarding school to do. I really had no idea what I'd do once I got there.

Days here, whatever they *are*, are not filled with the same sort of uncertainty that occupied my college era.

Between the normal humdrum of trying to survive in the heat, with the flies and bad food, there's the lingering knowledge that at any second one of my sergeants can come into the room and tell us to get our gear the fuck on, we've got to go. Our best time is three minutes—to throw on our body armor, load-carrying vest, and helmet, grab our weapons, and run out the door to our up-armored Humvees to respond to whatever crisis might erupt.

⁕

I remember sitting in UVA's Alderman Library stacks. I had twenty pages waiting to be filled with fleshed-out material from the couple of hundred note cards filled with citations, quotes, facts, and figures that all sat next to the computer. They sat there mockingly, a cluster of white paper bones waiting to be animated into a body. I had put an absurd amount of preparation into that paper—hours and hours in the library, on the phone, cruising databases, on the phone with sources, chewing through dusty old archives. All that work, all that preparation, for nothing. Twenty blank pages, all inconsequential pages. I remember thinking: *Why even bother?* All this preparation for something that will be read, halfheartedly, by a TA and then thrown away—another meaningless cluster of words carefully arranged and quickly forgotten. It seemed like a microcosm of my whole college career, a bunch of seemingly pointless preparations from grade school on up to receive a piece of parchment that signified nothing except that I can read, write, and show up to class on time. I was frustrated.

⁕

"Get your shit on and go to the trucks. Scouts got hit with an IED." The three guys from my platoon that I am eating with and I just look at each other for a second—then get up, leaving our trays, and run for the door. We run back to our barracks, half throw on our gear, and sprint out the front door to the truck still buckling and fastening straps.

"Radios on?" I ask, sliding into the back passenger seat, banging my M4 carbine and M203 grenade launcher against the seat's well.

"Yeah, they're good," our driver Bautista says as we pull out, while Burke is hopping into the turret behind the .50 caliber machine gun. "How's the FBCB2? Is it showing the screen?" I look up toward the computer monitor next to our lieutenant's seat, the glowing screen flickers to life and shows our map location as we move.

"Yeah, it's coming on."

"Fuck man."

"Yeah. Fuck."

•

Every Tuesday night on top of the dilapidated frat house was the same. James, Jon, me, and a case of Miller Light. James and Jon were both products of an exclusive Manhattan Jesuit high school, overeducated and neurotic. They half discussed, half debated Nietzsche and Heidegger every time we got together. I sat outside the conversation, gulped at my beer, looked at the stars, contributed comments here and there. I'd read those books, thought about them, written papers taking this position or that, but frankly, rants about the "thing unto itself" and the "ubermensch" weren't interesting, not tangible at all.

As we got progressively drunker, the talk of continental philosophy drifted a bit. Jon usually started playing his guitar; James ranted about his father, his girlfriend, the normal bitching. Beer cans accumulated around our feet and were crushed. Then I would stumble down the stairs and begin the long walk back to my apartment.

"Who's going to get Rashid?" We pull up in front of the Tactical Operation Center and Burke climbs out of the turret, jumping awkwardly off the hood while we are still moving, then stumbling toward our interpreter's room. Rashid, a twenty-three year old Afghani who picked up English while a refugee in Peshawar, comes running out toward our truck. We pass him his body armor and Soviet-made pistol, and then wait to roll out of the gate. My hands are shaking slightly as I put on my gloves.

"Who's got batteries?" Burke asks. The sun will be going down in a couple of hours, and scouts are about that far from our location, so anything we do in the next twelve hours will have to be through the greenish glow of our night vision goggles.

"Um...I've got four, plus two in my camera if we're desperate," I tell him.

                                                    *

Sara was the beautiful, smart, vivacious Cuban-American senior I'd had a crush on for the better part of my junior year. One day, half-drunk, I slipped a note through her mail slot. It was a note a week in the making—revised over and over, a perfect profession of love and devotion. I received her reply two days later, two pages of beautiful red lettering. Each perfectly formed consonant and vowel was a knife to the heart, each overly precise sentence ripped chunks out of my ego. It was hard to look at the whole letter, so I read it in disjointed pieces, trying to amuse myself by putting the puzzle together. I already knew what it said in so many words.

I had called James's cell phone and told him, wirelessly tethering my burden to him.

"Fuckin' sucks dude," he'd groaned. "She's a fuckin' bitch. Forget it. Me and Jon are smoking opium. Come over, it's pretty badass, feels like you're a couple of joints and a few Vicodin deep."

I hung up, drove back to my apartment, and demolished half a case of Heinekin while watching overdue videos until I passed out. My pillow was wet when I woke up.

●

I'd been cramming my brain for this one particular exam—up all night, wired on Red Bull and nicotine, shoving public policy readings long neglected into my short-term memory. The exam sat on the desk in front of me, a neatly typed-up sheet next to an open blue book. The first question was easy, I recall knowing that one. But after that my mind went blank. I stared. For an hour I stared like that, while pens scratched on paper all around me. I got up, turned in the empty blue book, and walked straight to my dean's office.

"Sir, I fucked up my exam. I'm not sure I can do this anymore."

Within the day, the paperwork was filed, stamped, and put away. Officially I'd withdrawn for the semester and taken a leave of absence from the university. The hardest part was telling my parents. I was a college dropout.

●

"Dammit, I didn't grab any snivel gear."

In my rush to get out to the trucks I hadn't grabbed any raincoats or fleece, nothing to keep me warm during the cold Afghani night. We sit up at the Tactical Operations Center awaiting permission from the battalion commander to enter the fray. We wait for ten minutes, which seems like an eternity, then twenty, and then an hour. We never actually get permission to go tonight and so we return to our rooms, shedding our dusty gear as the adrenaline seeps from our bodies.

●

Still in Virginia, but no longer in school, I had taken a job at Lowes, plotting my next move while hawking faucets and showerheads. That got old fast, naturally, but I really wasn't planning on going back to college for a while. The Army had always held a certain romantic appeal, even if I had decided West Point wasn't for me. Lowes was going nowhere, college was boring, and shit...why not?

So one day, coming home from work, I walked into an Army recruiter's office and signed up for three years as an infantryman. It had seemed like a logical decision—I'd get some adventure, get out of my head, and get away from, at least for a little while, my privileged white-boy roots for a life in which I was no more special than the next guy with an identical haircut and identical camouflage clothing.

I couldn't see anything else in the Army I wanted to do but pull a trigger, couldn't see myself repairing helicopters or decoding messages or anything like that. I just had the itch to carry all my gear on my back, strap a weapon to my front, and train to "close with and destroy the enemy." Who knows, maybe that enemy was myself.

WEIRDOES, WRITERS AND THE QUARTER-LIFE CRISIS

by Erika T. Wurth

Unlike most folks armed with a Ph.D., I come from a long line of manual laborers, criminals, and straight-up weirdoes. My grandparents, on both sides, worked at several jobs in their lives. My mother's father did liquor runs for the priests in Houston as a child to support his family, and later worked on a wharf, and much later raised his family as a park ranger, all of his kids working in the park as well. My mother's mother was a full-blooded Native American woman (Apache, Chickasaw, Cherokee). One of her first jobs was singing on a riverboat with her child from her first marriage, which was an arranged one. She was barely fifteen, and pregnant. The man she married was abusive and she left him. After marrying my mother's father at seventeen, she worked in different factories (where she lost her finger without any compensation). As an older woman, she worked as a janitor in my mother's high school to help send my mother to college. My mother and her sister were the first people in my family to not only go to college, but some of the first to graduate high school. My father's father was a fireman, and an airline pilot, and his mother worked at different department stores all of her life. They were married at nineteen.

My mother was told that she could be a nurse or a teacher *and* a homemaker. She chose teacher, but later in her life became the owner of a small dance studio, an extension of her dream as a child to become a movie star. My father was told that he was extremely intelligent and was provided scholarships, receiving his degree at Brooklyn Tech. He became an aerospace engineer, an extension of his dream as a child to be an astronaut. Both of my parents' childhood dreams were derived from television: my mother's—all of those crazy musicals; my father's—the movie *Superman*.

As you can imagine, although my parents found ways to weave their childhood dreams into their careers, they were taught to be largely pragmatic. And they were definitely inclined to teach their children to be the same way. Unfortunately for them their particular backgrounds backed up against their particular neuroses and their potential to give my sister and me a very different upbringing than their own, which resulted in the creation of two weird, little nerds. After all, my father was an eccentric, violent alcoholic who came from a long line of eccentric, violent alcoholics. My mother—who comes from a long line of thieves, pimps, hos, and generally crazy survivors—was told that the only way to escape the destiny of those who came before her was to assimilate into white culture at any cost.

My father spent all of his money, minus just enough to almost get us through, on alcohol, get-rich-quick schemes, and, later, women (like my mother's sleazy sister Kathy).

As far back as I can remember, he would bring home reams of lottery tickets, and he'd spend forever sitting at our ancient wooden table scraping away at the plasticy papery tickets, scratching and scratching away at his peculiar version of the American dream. For my birthday and for Christmas, he'd always give me a long line of lottery tickets.

Frequently, my father would sit me on his lap and extol the virtues of trickle-down economics, and, depending on whether I'd done my chores or not, would hand me my allowance. I'd put it in a jar and he'd hold it up to my nose. "Smell that," he'd say, and my mother would say, "Oh, Ron!" But she never stopped him.

My mother is a beautiful Indian woman with vetiligo, a disease that, patch by patch, takes away one's pigmentation. Originally, my mother had been a strong but easygoing woman. After twenty years of living with my father and his fists and alcohol, and a disease that robbed her of her most easy identification marker, my mother is less than at peace. She may have never sat me down on her lap and asked me to sniff the contents of glass jars, but she and I had our moments, moments that made their impressions upon me and what I was supposed to be like.

By the time I went to high school, I was a full-on weirdo. There were three of us weirdoes—you know, the three kids who, no matter what, you were above on the food chain. It was me, a slightly retarded dude who would ask every girl he met if they would go out with him, and Chipper Putfark. Yep, you heard right. Poor bastard. None of us were rich, but Chipper was poor, really poor. And he smelled. And he was orange headed (not red). And transparently pale. And freckled. *And* his family belonged to this really obscure religion (at least for us) that wouldn't allow him to participate in any holidays. And his name was *Chipper* freaking *Putfark*. At some point, he tried to make friends with me. I remember thinking that I wanted to say, "Look, Chipper, we get beat up enough alone, right? If we hang out, it'll be nerd power times ten."

The strange combination of privilege and oppression my parents had handed me, combined with my high school experience, had formed me. Not only had I been a total loner in high school but my high school hadn't exactly offered the standard American high school experience. My school was in a small town in the Rocky Mountains. The last time I visited, it appeared vaguely yuppie—yet another small mountain town to stop over in on your way to a ski resort. When *I* went to school there, it was an angry, blue-collar town with mainly working-class whites, and a handful of Mexicans and Indians.

For years I had eaten lunch under the display case, until my soon-to-be best friend Misty, another mixed-blood Native girl, took me by the hand (I think she was subconsciously afraid of how it would look for the race) and sat me down firmly at the nerd's table. Misty was tough and fantastic. I loved her even though, at times, she could be cruel. She had to be. Once the slightly retarded guy I mentioned earlier asked her out. She laughed at him until he disappeared. I didn't care. I was grateful to be eating lunch at a table. And yet I was still incredibly angry. And funny. But mainly just really fucking weird.

In college, I got better. I clearly remember sitting in the admissions office with a college counselor, silent, my parents talking about what I was going to study. They told her I was good at science, that I would major in something to do with that. I had objections, which I never voiced in public. But something about this woman, her sweet but slightly intellectual demeanor, made me feel like I could ask her the one question I knew I'd pay for. I cleared my voice and told her that I wanted to be a writer, and asked her what I could do with an English degree. I could feel the tension rising from my parents, the anger from both of them palpable. "No, no, she's not going to major in English," my father said, looking angry and threatening in my direction. "You can write on the side!" My mother hissed at me. This was her mantra.

The woman, who—as typical as this sounds—I remember now as young and blonde even if she wasn't, looked at my mother and then at my father the way I have to imagine she was forced to look at parents like mine five days a week. Then, she drew breath and said, "There are lots of things you can do with an English degree." My mother visibly recoiled and I could hear that growl sound my father always made under his breath. I smiled, my heart beating faster. "Like what?" I said. "Erika," my mother hissed and glanced over at me and back at the counselor. I felt like one of those kids on that movie *Goonies*, finally, finally on my way to the treasure, to what was surely going to save me, the thing that had to be the final secret to it all.

"You could be an editor, for example. Or a journalist. Or a teacher." I cocked my head. I really didn't know what an editor was, although it had vaguely writerly connotations that exited me. I knew what a journalist was though. Ugh. That shit that my father put up like a wall between his family and his face every freaking morning of my life with him. Forget it. And a teacher, well, I hated teachers. Or more precisely, they hated me. I was that weird kid in the back of class, always confused about the assignment in a school full of children who had even less to go on than I did. I was a continual source of irritation. Except to my English teachers. Come to think of it, they always loved me. "Teacher..." I said and she nodded and my parents directed the conversation away. But she had done it.

I was accepted into a public liberal arts college in the Rockies that same year. And from the beginning, it was everything that I wanted. I was away from my family, whom I loved but from whom I needed distance, away from my tough rural high school, and going to a small liberal arts school. It was an unimpressive college according to some, but I loved it. It was on traditional Indian ground, and as a result (and also due to its location) had two hundred and fifty represented tribes. There were other Indians, hippies, intellectuals, creative weirdoes: I was in heaven. And I wanted to be a writer. I had always wanted to be a writer, though I never knew why. I felt that it was a perfect place to start.

My first couple of weeks at school, I met a group of people, including a boy named Eric, who was half Japanese and half white. Eric was majoring in international business. I had put my major down as biology. After a week I knew that I definitely did not want things to get romantic between Eric and myself. He had the personality of a lima bean and never brushed his teeth. But boy, did that international business thing stick. I thought, oh, yeah, I could travel and make money and write...perfect life for a writer.

Then I took my first literature class. With Dr. Burns. Dr. Burns was about six foot six and had about four teeth that he never brushed, but this time I found that wildly appealing. As blatantly honest about sexuality as my mother and her sisters were, I was completely naïve, due to my father's repression and my own nerdiness. When Dr. Burns began to untie my shoelaces after the second class and asked me if I was going to let him continue to do it, I said yes. "You better be careful," he said, "you're going to end up half naked in the dean's office." I laughed.

Nothing ever happened. This isn't that kind of story.

As flirtatious as Burns was, he just wasn't going to pursue anything with anyone that didn't get it and didn't want it. The flirtation continued, however innocuously, and I couldn't run my ass fast enough to the administration's office to change my major from international business to English.

I felt guilty the whole way.

I also used to feel guilty when I masturbated. It's amazing how guilt never really stops you from doing the things you really like doing. A month later, my parents came to visit. I thought I'd get it over with in the hotel room before we went out to dinner, before my father had his first drink. I remember standing by the door, just in case, my mother sitting on the bed with my sister, my father by the desk.

"I'm majoring in English," I said. They were silent.

"You either have to change that or I'll take you out," my father said.

"Erika, you can write on the side!" My mother said and looked at me angrily, the subtext of everything that we ever talked about hung between us in the air, which was: You're going to make your father angry and then what will happen to us (we had tried to leave him when I was in third grade—it was a no go)? I went on to explain that there were things I could do with English, like be a journalist, or a teacher, or even just work a regular job. My parents argued. We went out to dinner. I never changed it and my father was too self-absorbed to really notice, my mother realized that she had been a teacher and so why couldn't I?

I didn't know until my third year in college that people could get Ph.D.s in things like English. In the town where I went to high school, there were more mullets than Ph.D.s—if there were *any* Ph.D.s. And with the exception of one of my auntie's husbands, nobody in my family had ever even come close to pursuing a Ph.D. In fact, during my program, one of my uncles would always ask me to look at his infected toe. I guess he thought I was becoming a medical doctor. Although when I tell this to my mother she always says, "Oh Christ, Erika! He asks everybody to look at his toe!"

I was in a Victorian literature class (I loved British literature—I had no interest in minority literature initially...it was way too close to home) when I met a girl named Karin who told me that I should join the writing group on campus and that she was going on with her degree in English and so should I. I thought about it. I did love my professors, and I was beginning to get the big picture that maybe a person could write on the side, but there wouldn't be a lot of time for it and it often destroyed people. And that a lot of writers were people from families who could support them, unlike mine. And that a lot of jobs were jobs that I would not enjoy or be good at, which was true—I've been fired from fourteen jobs in my life. I was realizing that as a creative writing teacher I would have a lot more time to write than most people, and I would be doing something I loved, and getting paid for it. And so I kept going. And going.

But I refused to take creative writing classes out of the sheer terror that someone would destroy my all too idealized portrayal of writing. Although at the time I said that it was because no one could tell me how to write—truly, I was chicken. I regret that. It would've been good for me and I would've learned about MFA programs—as it was, I was a year into my Ph.D. before I found out about them. However, I did complete a half-creative/half-critical dissertation (on American and specifically Native American and other American minority literature), and I have a job as a creative writing professor at a small university in Illinois (and I live in Iowa City, which rocks). I fought for that. I fought for everything: with my parents, with the people I worked for, with my dissertation committee, with people who feel that I'm too opinionated and ambitious. But I have what I want, which is time to write and a job that only furthers my love of writing. (There is nothing, and I mean nothing, more honest than a room full of nineteen year olds talking about a book and why it sucks. I have cringed for writers.) I am now thirty years old.

And when I look back, there were crises—romantic (first love abandoning me and being kidnapped by paramilitary troopers), family (one of my cousins stole a train), and personal (I pissed the wrong people off). And I am in serious debt now. But I knew what I wanted.

There are other stories like mine, that, at first glance, seem to typify the worst aspects of the quarter-life crisis/post-Gen-X stereotype, novels like *A Heartbreaking Work of Staggering Genius*, *White Teeth*, *The Namesake*, and countless others...novels and memoirs expressing the angst of people in the prime of their lives, living in ridiculously overindulged, wealthy countries from authors that don't always come from overindulged backgrounds. That's why I love them. Because, for the most part, they're not really about the authors' mid-twenties crises either—at least, not in any typical way. They're often stories much like mine, stories about people who were determined to take the risk.

part:

2

GOODBYE SOUL,
HELLO BACON

The juxtaposition of a busy college schedule and nothing-really-to-do doldrums is harsh. Just a few months ago, we were studying for finals, writing wow-'em papers, attending receptions and parties, and now, well, now our lives aren't quite so full. "But I've got this great degree!" "But I'm so well qualified!" "I'm special!" The energy that goes into the post-college job search quickly turns to anger and then apathy. Suddenly an amped-up Tigger becomes a grumbling Eeyore. "I'm never going to get a job." "I'm a loser."

We've all heard the self-help platitudes ("Do what you love." "Don't take that job with all the perks if it doesn't *do it* for you."), but we're not really listening, are we? It's not like most dream jobs, ready with six-figure salaries and corporate expense accounts, are calling for twentysomethings. And aren't there fields of work that have to get done but don't *do it* for anyone? What about those times when there are just no jobs to be had, at all?

Still we all eventually plod off, ready to take our place with that first job that lies somewhere between our ideal and our worst nightmare. So how exactly does that happen, especially for those of us who hate job hunting and, worse, working in general? Naturally, the first step is discovering what does "do it for you," and, naturally, for most people this first step is a doozy. With only the classifieds for comfort, most of us patch together resumes, use the fire-as-many-bullets-as-you-can method, and work the crappiest of crappy gigs, letting fate more or less set the course.

For those of us lucky enough to figure out how to bring home the turkey bacon, souls intact, we still have to get through the dreaded interview. "Arrive fifteen minutes early." "Sell yourself." "Firmly shake your interviewer's hand." Yes, tell the interviewer how you can't wait to take your place on cubicle row for a job that barely covers rent. And remember, whatever meager amount of self-esteem you had will likely be crushed as you recognize your worth in some middle-manager's eyes.

And then we go out and do it all again tomorrow.

Maybe it's not such a bad idea to arm ourselves with some tidy advice after all.

HAILING   A CAB

by *Catherine Strawn*

Really, could that have gone any worse? I thought as I stepped out onto the sidewalk, walked to the edge, and uneasily held up my arm to hail a cab. It was the second I'd hailed in my life.

"LaGuardia, please." I didn't need to leave for the airport this early, but I was cowering with shame. I'd just had the most awful interview and wanted to be back in Chicago, where I knew north from south and I didn't need to know a location's cross street to get where I wanted to go.

After three days of endless smiling through interview after interview, my clothes were filled with perspiration from 100-degree weather and I felt completely deflated. Some interviewers seemed nice, and a couple even acted impressed, but none were dying to snap me up and put my genius to work. It was hard to conjure up a little confidence when no one wanted to employ me. I mean, it wasn't like I'd be raising their first-born child.

Interviewing is like flirting, except that if an interviewer's not interested, he can't just walk away, disappearing into a crowded bar. Human resources doesn't say, "I'm sorry, Catherine. You're just not my type, but I think your friend's pretty cute." So in this last, wretched interview, when someone acted openly disinterested, I was caught off guard. Really, I should have been pleased with her honesty, but instead I was shocked, and I left feeling even more self-conscious.

"What was your favorite story in the last issue?" she had asked. Studying back issues of all the magazines published by three huge companies had left me a little confused. I thought, *I can't think of a single story that was in the last issue, let alone one I actually liked.* Plus, there was no way I could have generated a coherent, intelligent response with someone looking at me with an expression that said, *I don't have time for this. I'm way too important, and these five minutes are my gift to you.*

As she coolly stared me down, I fumbled to say something. Her response, a scowl, made me wonder whether she was having a bad day or if that was her usual facial expression. And even though her style had clearly called in sick that day, I didn't feel comfortable with my Old Navy shirt or myself, though thankfully I did know enough not to wear a Guadalajara poncho, *Ugly Betty*–style.

"So, tell me about yourself."

"Well, I grew up in Canton, Ohio, home of the Pro Football Hall of Fame (my standard icebreaker), and I just finished journalism school at Northwestern..." She did not find this information of interest and felt she needed to remind me *again* that the position was in the fashion department; I would never write a word for the magazine and instead I would keep track of clothes made by designers whose names I couldn't even pronounce.

"What do you like and dislike about the magazine?"

"The clothes seem very wearable, like outfits readers would actually put on for a day at work. As for the writing,

I really relate to the first-person essays. But, I wish there weren't so many stories on dieting. Maybe it's because I'm younger and don't think about losing weight as much, but it seems like dieting articles just make women feel bad about themselves." *Hmmm...perhaps that wasn't the best answer,* I thought, immediately regretting my candor. *Was I too harsh?*

I spent the entire interview wishing I could walk out and mollify myself with some French fries, so I was relieved when she finally said, "Do you have any questions for me?" thus concluding the interview. I thought about asking a follow up, such as "What's the office environment like?" but she had already given me a clear picture of what life there would be like. Really, I was pretty lucky she hadn't asked me my favorite designers. Obviously fashion wasn't my specialty, and I didn't have a clue whose fall collections were standouts.

She devoured me in approximately twenty minutes, which was why I was getting into a cab more than three hours before my flight was scheduled to leave.

This three-day trip was supposed to be my big introduction to the New York City magazine world. But in the weeks leading up to the interviews, I started feeling anxious, had trouble sleeping, and chewed my nails—and I hadn't bitten my nails since taking AP tests in high school. I grew even more paranoid when my dad convinced me that interviewers would take one look at my short nails and realize I didn't have my shit together. Great.

The search certainly hadn't gone as well as I had hoped, and I couldn't move to New York without a job— to my parents that was unheard of. Actually, my dad thought the companies should be paying to fly me out if they wanted to interview me. That may happen in investment banking but not in magazine publishing. I didn't even know if I could afford to come back to New York for more interviews, and there I was, leaving without a single lead toward a job.

On the other hand, my parents had always been supportive about letting me pursue the career I wanted. From the time I was in middle school and my dad helped with pre-Algebra homework, he would always tell me how he wished he had become a high school math teacher—and that meant a lot coming from a high-powered attorney. I've always known I didn't have to become a doctor to make my parents happy or proud. They just didn't think I'd be able to live in New York and support myself when I told them how much I'd be making. (Barely enough to feed myself...luckily, I love peanut butter and jelly sandwiches.)

Several years prior to this, long before it had sunk in that I eventually would have to get a job, my mom decided to go back to work. She'd raised three children, run four marathons, and been the president of the local hospital's women's board, among other things, and she still came home from interviews sighing with rejection. She came back one afternoon from another unsuccessful interview, and we sat at the kitchen table while she told me how she'd been stumped by the interviewer's question about her long-range career goals. I wondered how they could reduce her confidence to nothing. What is it about interviewing that makes everyone nervous, no matter how experienced or well spoken?

All of a sudden my cell phone rang—"unidentified caller" came up on caller ID. Only my best friend from high school and the uptight bitch I had just interviewed with come up on my phone as "unidentified caller." I hoped it would be the former, but it was neither.

"Hi, this is Cheryl from *Jane Magazine*. I just got your resume and was wondering if you'd be interested in interviewing for a job."

"Of course! Only I'm on my way to the airport to go back to Chicago and won't be back for two weeks. Could I interview then?"

"Sure," she said. "I don't know what our timeframe is for filling the position, but definitely call me when you're back in town." This response was surprising. Magazine jobs fill in a matter of nanoseconds.

Clearly, I was still rattled from the hideous answers that had come out of my mouth half an hour earlier. But what was I going to do, have the driver do a U-turn on the Triborough Bridge? Once I arrived at the airport, I came to terms with my stupidity and realized I needed to get back and interview immediately. A job like this, or even circumstances where people want to meet with you, don't come along too often.

I called the company's main number, tracked down Cheryl, and told her I could come in to interview immediately. Thankfully, I hadn't changed into my "flying" sweats for the flight and was still wearing the outfit I'd worn to the awful interview; however, I was a little worried that my professional attire would seem a little stuffy for *Jane*. Didn't I bring any jewelry to make my Old Navy shirt and Banana Republic skirt a little more...funky? I looked more like I was going to work at a bank than an environment where creativity is valued, but there was no time to change.

What do you know about the magazine, who are your favorite writers, what are your strengths and weaknesses? I started thinking about possible answers to the usual questions. Ironically, I had just left behind all of the magazines I had been studying—they were too heavy to carry around. So I sat nervously in the back seat of the cab, quietly going through the magazine's different sections in my mind and thinking about what I liked most and what made it different from competitors. It helped that I completely adored the magazine, so there'd be no need to lie.

Half an hour later, the cab dropped me back off at the corner of 34th Street and 5th Avenue. Meeting with Cheryl was like catching up with a chatty high school friend. Sometimes I can be shy, but with Cheryl gabbing away, I opened up and I became pretty talkative, too. We got to know each other. It wasn't all her questions and my answers though. I learned about her, too. She commuted from her parents' house in Philadelphia before moving to New York. She was in a sorority in college. She, and everyone else just starting out in magazines, had learned how to survive on her less-than impressive salary and the occasional free beauty product.

After spending an hour talking with Cheryl and Cheryl's boss, I hopped into another cab and rode back to the airport, making it onto the next flight to Chicago. To my absolute pleasure, I started working at *Jane* the day after I finished school. But the truth is, the interviewing doesn't ever stop; I'd seen my mom, for one, face inane interrogations about her long-range career goals. Someday I'll have to go back out there and tell people about my "strengths and weaknesses" and how I've overcome them. I may even come across that particularly unfriendly interviewer and flame out once again. But at least now I know how to say hard-to-pronounce designer names like Proenza Schouler, you know, in case anyone asks.

HOW I BECAME A BED-MAKER

by *Kate Torgovnick*

I realized a very scary thing this morning: I've become the kind of person who makes their bed every day. I woke up to the evil buzzing of my alarm clock, like always. And as I came out of that two minutes of post-sleep daze, I found myself at the end of my bed, wrestling to get the lines of my comforter parallel to the edge of my mattress.

I, Kate Torgovnick, make my bed every morning. *Every* morning. Not just days when friends might be coming over or days when I've done the laundry and need to change my sheets—we're talking every weekday, weekend, and holiday. It doesn't matter if I'm running late for work or if I have a hangover from too many gin and tonics the night before. No matter what, I make my bed.

And I'm not just talking about the throwing of covers over everything and thinking, *The bed is done, man, the bed is* done, like that kid with the long hair in *Don't Tell Mom the Babysitter's Dead* would say. I make my bed in a way that would please any drill sergeant. First, I fluff each sham (I don't even know where I picked up this term) and prop it up against my headboard, making sure no edges are flopping over. Then I shake out both of my pillows. I tuck three sides of the top sheet—yes, there's a *top sheet*—between the mattress and box spring and pull the loose end over my pillows. Next, I attack the comforter. I pull it over the whole kit and caboodle and take at least a minute to straighten it out (this was the point I was at when I came to this awful, dizzying realization this morning). Oh, but we're not done yet. Next, at the head of the bed, I fold the top sheet and comforter down about four inches, the way maids in hotels are taught to do. Finally, from the right side of the bed where I've neatly stacked my toss pillows, I grab each one individually and arrange them big ones in the back, small ones in the front. I've developed a meticulous process that takes approximately four minutes to complete—yet until today, I never even realized that I do any of it at all.

How could this have happened? Trust me, I am *not* a bed-maker. Or, at least, I wasn't a bed-maker? I like to think of myself as laid back, cool, smart, funny, and not nearly compulsive enough to attend to the details listed above. I'm hardly someone you would call organized—I've barely touched the day planner I bought years ago and instead jot my appointments down on paper scraps that become a jumbled mess at the bottom of my purse. I pay my bills late and they're often stained with jelly. As a teenager, my room was messy with the requisite piles of clothing, mix tapes, and the occasional abandoned cupcake. I actually remember making fun of my parents for their always-made bed. My freshman dorm room was a respectable pig sty—the floor a sea of crumpled jeans, half-written papers, and trash I couldn't be bothered to bring to a trash can. Nowhere in my life has bed-making ever entered into the equation. So when did this happen?

First step, I must figure out how long this bed-making has been going on. It's 8:30 a.m., but I panic and call my boyfriend, Chuck. After three long rings, he finally picks up. "Hey," he says, his voice betraying that I'm calling well before his alarm clock. "Everything okay?" I try to think of the best way to phrase this. "Have you noticed that I make my bed?" I ask.

I hear a relieved sigh on the other end of the line. He seems thankful that the serious note in my voice is not anything bad. "Um...yeah."

"How long have I been doing this?" I delve. "Do you remember when it started?"

He pauses for a minute. "You've always made your bed. At least since we've been together."

Wow. That's three years. How can someone make their bed every day for three years and not even notice? I snap back into the conversation. "Did you ever think that's a little strange?"

"Not really," he says. "I mean, that's pretty normal. Lots of people do it."

"Well, have there been any days when I haven't made my bed?" I ask in a last-ditch effort.

He thinks. "Not that I can remember. You even make my bed when you're over here." Crap. My bed-making's practically turning me into a fifties housewife.

I say goodbye and do the math in my head. It must have been sometime pre-2004 when the bed-making began. That narrows it down, but doesn't answer the question. I guess I'm going to have to dig back further.

I try calling Christina, my post-college roommate who I lived with for three years before moving into my own studio, but she's not picking up her phone. So I instant message Dana, my college roommate. Maybe she saw the first symptoms. "Hey there," I say. "Do you ever remember me making my bed?"

"No way," she messages back. "I don't think so."

"So I was a slob? On a scale of 1 to 10, how messy was my side of the room?"

"If 1 is a monk's cell and 10 is Britney Spears' career, it was an 8.5. But by senior year, maybe a 6," she offers. Bless her for her bluntness. "But it still looked like you had artfully planned to make sure no horizontal surface was exposed, be it floor, chair, bed, or desk." Maybe she is exaggerating (this is someone who would get annoyed if the toilet paper roll was placed on the holder with the end coming out underneath instead of over the top). But she's narrowed down the time frame considerably. Somewhere between graduating from college in 2002 and getting together with Chuck in 2004, the bed-making began.

Christina is the missing link. Thankfully, she calls back a few hours later. "Do you remember when I started making my bed?" I ask, completely forgetting the normal pleasantries.

She laughs. "Not really."

"Did I ever mention making my bed or anything like that?"

"Hmm...not that I can remember," she says.

"Sorry, I realized today that I make my bed every day, and I'm trying to figure out when that started," I say, suddenly aware that I'm sounding like a psycho.

"That's funny," she says. "I've started making my bed, too. In our old apartment I didn't care about it. But in my new apartment, my bed's in the middle of the room. If I don't make it in the morning, I come home and feel like my life is a mess."

This is inconceivable. Christina's now a bed-maker, too? Her room was always twice as messy as mine—mountains of clothes on the floor, books strewn every which way, the works. Is what I'm going though completely normal?

"Really?" I say, feeling calmed that she's going through this, too. "Well, do you ever remember me going on any cleaning spurts or anything like that?"

"When we were both looking for jobs, you'd go on cleaning kicks or resolve to organize the closet or something. Maybe it was then?" she offers. And all of a sudden, I remember. I started making my bed in the fall of 2002. It makes sense now that I think about it—I was unemployed for months and probably would have slept all day had I not forced myself out of bed. Christina was in the unemployed trenches with me, but our third roommate, Susannah, was two years older than us and had a steady job. In the morning, she would always make her bed before leaving the apartment for work. In the evening, she'd casually tell us about the things she did at the office, and I'd feel embarrassed that the only thing I had to report on was whether Joey and Dawson hooked up in the day's episode of *Dawson's Creek*. So maybe I was copying Susannah, imitating what productive members of society do.

Or maybe I was trying to establish some sort of routine. I remember giving myself a schedule so I didn't fall too out of practice with having things to do. 10 a.m.: the aforementioned *Creek*. 11 a.m.: take a shower and get dressed. Noon: look for a job for an hour. 1 p.m.: Go to the grocery store and make lunch. 2 p.m.: five hours of *Law and Order* reruns. 7 p.m.: Call friends and come up with a plan for the night that didn't involve spending money. I remember one day during this period when the building across the street caught on fire. I noticed the smoke through our bay window just as the fire trucks came into view. I stood there for hours, watching as flames engulfed the building and it burned down to the ground. It never even crossed my mind to go see if anyone needed my help. No one was injured, so it's not as creepy as it sounds—but still, I consider this a low point. The fire seemed metaphorical for how power-less I was feeling at the time. Four years at a highly ranked liberal arts college making Phi Beta Kappa and Summa Cum Laude, and I felt completely ineffectual in shaping my life. Just like the firefighters' hoses did nothing to calm the flames. Looking back, I think maybe my bed-making was my way of taking control of something. I couldn't find a job, not to mention a boyfriend, and my savings account had dwindled to nothing. But if I made my bed, I was the master of my universe, right?

But why do I continue this obscene behavior now that life has settled down—I've found my dream job, I'm half-way through writing my first book, and all and all I'm very pleased with my life? I can think of all sorts of logi-cal reasons. I could say that it helps me wake up, explicitly defining that the night is over and that, as much as I might want to, I can't go back to bed. I could say that coming home to a neat bed after work makes me feel mentally in order. I could say, "Cleanliness is godliness," or some such quote that doesn't really make much sense. And while there might be an ounce of truth in these things, I think that there is more to it than that: I think that my unconscious bed-making means I'm truly an adult.

I've heard friends and coworkers utter the phrase, "pretending to be an adult," and until now I've completely understood the sentiment. This state of perpetual responsi-bility feels foreign to all of us. We all feel like we're acting out a part—playing dress-up and doing things we're sup-posed to do, like going to work and setting up 401Ks, but that these things never seem completely natural. In this way of thinking, being an adult is measured in firsts you never quite imagined you'd get to—your first apartment, your first job, the first time someone calls you "Ma'am," the first paycheck that reflects a salary and not an hourly rate, the first time you say "I'll pencil you in," the first property you own, the first birthday cake with number candles rather than individual ones, the first time you think about getting married and having children and it doesn't seem completely far-fetched. But I've been through every one of these milestones, and, while they sound big on paper, the truth is that I felt no different on the day before any of these things happened than I did on the day after.

But today, the day I realized that I am a bed-maker, I feel very, very different. See, I've come to realize that adulthood is a diffuse thing. It creeps up in the subtlest ways possible. It's making to-do lists on a regular basis instead of just doing things. It's getting annoyed at shows when people bump into you when you use to think that was big fun. It's no longer telling your friends to just come on over, but giving them a specific time to arrive so that you can clean up and make a cheese plate (preferably with grapes). Adultness seeps into the tiniest crevices of your everyday life, to the point where you don't even recognize it. It seems so natural that you can't pin it down. It's when stability and routine become the things you really want. When having the wildest-night-ever pales in comparison to the simple pleasure of untucking the comforter, crawling inside, pulling the sheet all the way up to your neck, and drifting off to sleep.

I know I have friends who'd be willing to stage an intervention to try to shake me free from making my bed. Maybe there's even a twelve-step program. But the truth is, I don't want to stop. I like the way this ritual feels— easy, small, and comforting. Sure, I don't ever want to be grown up to the point where the phrase "bed-maker" seems like a fitting way to describe myself. But I can accept this. I can accept that I make my bed every day, that I'm an adult, that my priorities are shifting, that there is no Never, Never Land.

I have to go now. Toss pillows to rearrange.

HOW TO GET A JOB AND SURVIVE THE QLC WITH DIGNITY, HONOR, AND THE AMERICAN WAY

by Harmon Leon

Hello, one-quarter-aged-Americans! In our rich, fat country of wealth and opportunity, we are given the extravagance of suffering through career indecision.

"I don't know what to do with my life!" say you who are going through this. "I have too many options!" Finding your true calling can be a challenge, even for the most competent of our generation. Even I had difficulty deciding upon which surface I should shine my brilliant light. Yet, despite my many, many setbacks (and strange rashes), I overcame. And you can, too.

It's not just a twenty-first century thing. Many famous people throughout history have themselves suffered a quarter-life crisis. For example, French scientist Madame Curie didn't know what to do with her life. After a couple of failed jobs in the late 1800s, she took a gig as a tutor. But soon she started messing around with radiation. Look where that got her, a Nobel Prize in physics and chemistry! (Note: Curie later died due to excessive exposure to radiation.)

One of the worst cases of quarter-life crisis, though, has got to be that of young Orson Wells. At the age of twenty-five, Orson Wells—whom many considered the Ben Affleck of his day—wrote, starred in, and directed *Citizen Kane*. The instant movie classic is a psychological study of an American newspaper tycoon whose life pursuit to obtain his childhood sled, *Rosebud*, eventually drove him mad. Here was a man who reached the pinnacle of wealth, yet could never again attain the carefree innocence of his youth. The point: sledding is awesome.

Alas, Mr. Well's meteoric early success merely forestalled his naturally occurring quarter-life crisis, which emerged forty years later as a late-life crisis. The lesson to be learned from Mr. Big-and-Clever Citizen Kane is that your quarter-life crises should happen while you are still young and sexy and have time to stage a comeback. Thus you can avoid being known as the classic example of a genius that burns early in life only to flicker and fade later on while turning very rotund and hawking cheap wine on TV commercials. The key is pacing.

Like lots of young people of today, Will Smith felt like his various interests were pulling him in different directions. Fortunately, for the good of humanity, the wacky Philadelphia MC teamed up with Jazzy Jeff in order to create the hit song "Parents Just Don't Understand." This eventually led to his starring role in *The Fresh Prince of Bel Air*. A classic fish-out-of-water tale, the mid nineties sitcom was credited with healing class and race relations in our country, such as the episode where Will and Carlton trick the bulter Geoffrey into thinking he won the lottery. Hilarious—yet poignant. Smith went on to star in *Hitch*, a movie about a professional date doctor who finds himself questioning his shallow existance and learns to love. The rest is quarter-life-crisis-resolution history!

As all of these personalities display, all of *us* have the ability to overcome the quarter-life crisis and become productive members of society. (Except for you with the thick eyebrows. You're totally fucked.) So quit your damn whining. It could be a hell of a lot worse.

As for me, all I can say is that it was a good thing I didn't peak early and suffer a quarter-life meltdown in my pursuit of being America's favorite infiltrator. Yes, it was a bit of a rough path. What could I do but make a living embracing my one true talent of scribbling nonsense in notebooks? The naysayers sneered, "You can't pay the bills on the laughter of children or the smiles of the elderly."

"But I can," I retorted, "and I shall!" When my outlook appeared to be at its darkest, I stuck to my mission (whatever it was) and overcame. Here are a few highlights from the depths to which I plunged while scouring the murky bottom of twentysomethinghood.

●

QUARTER-LIFE CRISIS VOCATION
Human-Sized Subway Sandwich

Location: Assorted street corners in downtown San Francisco

Job Description: Distributing discount flyers for Subway sandwiches to people who were in arms length of me, dressed as a human-sized Subway sandwich.

Duration: Two days; it was described as an "acting job," when in reality it felt not unlike being the village idiot.

Benefits: None, unless you count being openly ridiculed a benefit.

Disadvantages: Passersby avoided me like dog shit. Made me contemplate my true purpose in life. I also developed empathy for dog shit.

•

QUARTER-LIFE CRISIS ROOMMATES
Matt and Susanna

Duration: Five months

Occupations: Catering

Slobs or Neat Freaks: Neat freaks; a strict rule was enforced about scrubbing out the bathtub after taking a shower.

Weird Quirks: Obsessive about the arrangement of cans on their food shelf. Peas and string beans were not allowed to fraternize. Also, they would laugh uproariously at *America's Funniest Home Videos.*

Tension Turning Point: A friend of mine used Matt's towel after a shower. My roommate didn't speak to me for three days.

Act of Revenge: I ate some of their food and began a complete roommate-duty boycott that included: not taking phone messages, refusal to take out the trash, and a parade of loud friends late at night.

End Result: An intense volley of nasty, handwritten notes. When I moved in, I was friends with both Matt and Susanna. After moving out, only one of the two will engage me in verbal communication. To this day, I cannot wipe down a bathtub without weeping.

QUARTER-LIFE CRISIS GIRLFRIEND
Aileen Wournos (blatant name change)

Profile: Ex-stripper with a cocaine problem of frequent-bloody-nose proportions, who lacked any sort of directional motivation and moved in with me on our second date.

Duration of Relationship: 3 1/2 years

Reason for Attraction: Aside from being wicked hot, she claimed to be artistic, which she never demonstrated at any point.

High Points: I always had someone to party with.

Low Points: I always had someone to party with.

How It Ended: After she was canned from her waitress job because of her drug-addled insanity, we broke up. Her next grand life step was moving back to Canada to live with her mom. (Me bitter? No.)

Girlfriend Rating: 1/2 star

OPTIONS FOR THOSE HAVING OR WISHING FOR A QUARTER-LIFE CRISIS

• Go backpacking through the state of Delaware.

• Break a Guinness Book of World Records record.

- Stalk celebrities.

- Become a sharpshooter of rats down by the river.

- Bare-knuckle box for quarters down by the dock.

- Become a superhero by claiming to have X-ray vision.

- Learn TV repair at Devry Institute.

- Get a sweet neck tattoo of Abe Lincoln—complete with stovepipe hat.

- Start a pancake-eating contest for senior citizens.

- Star in driver's-ed films.

- Develop a limp and have people call you "Limpy."

- Grow facial hair and get food stuck in it.

- Learn Finnish.

- Take up the washboard in your local junkyard band.

- **Turn to drugs and alcohol in order to "reinvent yourself."**

- Buy a shiny red sports car with last night's tip money.

·

What brought me though my quarter-life crisis was a strong commitment to my goals. My road seemed rocky, my ladder was slippery, my elevator was, at times, shut down for maintenance. Many jobs ended badly: parking valet, airport shuttle-van driver, bartender, waiter, landscaper, telemarketer, bike-cab driver, turkey farmer, food delivery guy. It's the dirt under my fingernails, and the dissatisfaction thereof, which led me to my life's holy pursuit of sticking it to *The Man!* By putting it all into global and historical perspective, it doesn't seem so bad. Be it a different era, a quarter-life crisis would take on a harsher, not to mention darker, tone. If, say, you were having a quarter-life crisis in fourteenth-century Europe, your quarter-life crisis would not center around whether you should go to graduate school and get that degree in (insert name of funny-thing-to-get-graduate-degree-in here) _____. No. Contracting the bubonic plague would be one of your prime, quarter-life-crisis concerns. That's right, your quarter-life crisis would be centered on whether or not you'd be bricked up in your house by the local villagers while blood streams from every orifice of your body. So, cheer up. Moving back in with your parents only *feels* that bad.

AFTERLIFE

It was the year after I graduated college and I was touring with my band. We had purchased a van that ran on the meager earnings of sets played to half-full bars in places like Ypsilanti, Michigan. Barreling down randomly numbered highways, there was always a feeling of death in the air because no matter what anyone tells you there are only a handful of stories in the world, and one of them is about dying young, about chasing your dream off the edge of a cliff.

There were times that I dreamed epic car-crash dreams while sleeping in the back of that van. It didn't help that I once asked my band mates which of us they thought would die first and they simultaneously responded "You," like they'd been waiting to say it since the day we met.

Cutting into my thoughts about death was a boy I said I loved. The distance of touring made him an outline, a face I could hardly picture during late-night phone calls from the dead rural space between Midwest cities. The boy spent three months in Los Angeles with a film director who'd crowned himself the "Patron Fag of West Hollywood," a director with an Aston Martin and an underfurnished house in the hills. Conversations with the boy ended with him saying things like, "Okay, I have to get in the hot tub now" and "I think someone slipped something in my drink." Other times the line just went dead, like someone had grabbed his phone and hung it up. These are not the things you want to deal with while floating through the darkened landscape at 4 a.m. with $8.75 in your checking account and Lou Reed droning on about heroin.

Our band had songs on MTV. Not videos, but clips of songs played during reality shows where awful people did awful things to each other for vacations, prepaid credit cards, or just the chance to have their horribleness televised on basic cable. One of our songs played while two girls wrestled for a boy on an early episode of *Sorority Life*. I wrote that song. It was about how hanging myself wouldn't fix the fact that my first real boyfriend had dumped me; then it became the soundtrack for a different kind of heartbreak, the kind that lost its value the moment the advertisers pulled out their checkbooks.

But we thought we were going somewhere. Sometimes a venue was full of people, for no discernable reason except that kids in that town had nothing better to do on a Friday night then see a band they'd heard on college radio a few times. So much of that time on the road went beyond the realm of mystery and traveled into ghost story territory, like the time I walked into a bar in a city I'd never been to before and saw "NICK BURD IS AN ASSHOLE" written on one of the posters we'd sent the club a few weeks before. I wondered if we'd already played this show, already sucked, already pissed someone off.

The phone calls from home collected like change in my pocket. My mother wanted to know when I was coming home, when I was going to call my student loan officer and explain why I wasn't paying off the thousands of .dollars of debt I'd acquired for the sake of an English degree. "We're going to blow up soon," I said. "I can feel it. People are buying the album, singing along with the words. By next summer I'll be living in Los Angels in some mansion that a record company bought for the band. We'll write our second album on the beach. I'll break up with the boy and write a million songs about it. I'll go to the Gap and get attacked by hordes of screaming girls, and it'll be so easy to look disinterested and that will only make them crazier, make them buy more copies of the album. I'll be the first openly gay pop icon, sort of like George Michael but without the self-destructive neurosis. I'll be just like that line in the song of ours where I say: 'I'll prove you wrong by doing right.' I'll do good, Mom. I promise. Just you wait and see."

And she believed this. Everyone believed this—Kathryn, our bass player; Matt, the drummer; even Chris, our pragmatic lead guitarist who had no qualms about calling out bullshit when he smelled it. Our families, our friends, they all had faith. In fact, everyone close to us believed wholeheartedly in the religion of our band, everyone except me. And it wasn't because we were bad or inept or doomed. I believed in my band mates' abilities, in their work ethic, and in their love of music that crossed the border into fanaticism. It was myself that I didn't believe in. I had trouble believing for the same reasons as any other creature: low self-esteem, a distorted sense of how the world worked. I thought I was a shitty guitarist, that my lyrics didn't quite ring true. I could never find the right chord, the right line. My metaphors were sloppy. I didn't bounce around enough when the chorus got loud. The hipsters in our hometown of Iowa City found us too poppy, too commercial, and I let their jaded stares affect me, let them dictate who I was. To this day I wonder if a good drug habit or an inflated ego would have actually done me some good, could have maybe catapulted me into having a faith in myself that no naysayer could bust.

But it was hard to find faith at the end of the evening when we made the rounds of whatever bar we were playing in and begged strangers to let us sleep on their floor and eat their food. Someone almost always took us home, save for the evening in Asbury Park when we parked the van on the beach and slept in the back as the tail of a hurricane swept in and shook our van. But the van was never my home, which is what I wanted more than anything.

Maybe I wouldn't have been so obsessed with the idea of home if I'd actually had a home back in Iowa. My mother had moved in with a man who would be my stepfather for all of six months, and their house was in a town I hadn't grown up in, a town where people leaned out of their cars and screamed *nigger* at me when I walked through the three-block area they sarcastically referred to as downtown. During gaps in touring I would stay at this new house, unable to find a light switch in a darkened room. I'd call my stepfather at work and ask how to work the big-screen television or the hot tub, both purchases my mother made in the week after I left home for college that made me wonder if she was subconsciously replacing me with stuff.

The time between touring felt like time off from a series of missions to space. I had come to Earth to eat her food and abuse my mother's Pay-Per-View, but within days I would climb back on the shuttle and blast off to a place where there was no such thing as gravity. I would be wandering around the kitchen looking for the switch that turned on the garbage disposal, thinking: *If my mother always said she'd never live in a fucking ranch-style house, why am I wandering around her ranch-style house?* All this domestic/road contemplation with my ears ringing from twenty evenings of my amp being turned up too loud was too much.

I began to associate certain smells and tastes and songs with various aspects of touring. Red Bull tasted like everyone in the van was asleep, and I was the one in charge of getting us to our next show in one piece. CK One was me working the merch table and trying to explain how a delay pedal worked to a drunk frat boy wearing too much cologne while my band mates flirted with members of the opposite sex in various corners of the bar. R.E.M.'s "Be Mine" was me buying drinks I couldn't afford for a sexually ambiguous boy in Chicago who wanted to talk about Marxism instead of blowjobs, the one whose girl-friend showed up just as I was getting up the courage to lean in and kiss him, the one who said "see ya' around" before I never saw him again.

Somehow I found something to associate with home. We had a few days off on the East Coast, and we spent them with our bass player's sister in New York City. We were sitting in her apartment and drinking her booze when I blurted out, "I want to live here," and suddenly all I could think about was moving to Manhattan. I dreamt of being an anonymous face on the street, someone without a past, a man in a self-imposed witness relocation pro-gram. I could make up details, a new name even. I could turn myself into someone better than who I actually was.

I came back to Iowa and immediately applied for graduate schools in New York. All this was done in secret because I'd only hinted at the idea of escaping Iowa, but none of my band mates were ready for that. It was something I would have to do on my own, and even though it was terrifying, I was happy for that. In fact, it felt like the only way to do it was to do it by myself, because my entire life until then had been all about me traveling in a pack where I wasn't allowed to have the final say. In retrospect, the one thing about band life that I had the hardest time dealing with was having to deal with other people's input, having to bend what I wanted into what was best for everyone. My dream of New York carried doubts, carried the idea that I would finally fail on my own and be forced to bear the consequences of a faulty life all by myself, but even that sounded like a good escape to me. I'd always been selfish, even when it came to taking all the blame.

We stopped touring for a while, stopped to work jobs, save up more money. It was good to go more than three days without having to succumb to the McDonald's dollar menu for a meal that was an amalgamation of breakfast, lunch, and dinner. Even the windowless room in my mother's basement where I slept felt like a luxury, at least during the first few days back. During the day I worked the service counter at my stepfather's grocery store where I got to deal with a seemingly never-ending string of people trying to buy lottery tickets with their food stamps and my stepfather's business partner referring to me as "Blackie" during his late-night visits for that second pint of vodka. Customers would ask, "If you graduated college, why are you working in a grocery store?" At first my line was: "It was a dream, and I made it happen." But after a while I just shrugged, mumbled something about being in a band, and threw their receipt in the bag.

On some days I forgot I was in a band. I would pick up my guitar and play a G-chord over and over again until it felt like that was the only sound in the world, like it was the lung through which all songs breathed. Then I would put it back in its case like a pet I secretly wished would die. Even my love for listening to music died. Every album I owned was a document proving someone else's success, and the jealousy made my throat constrict, made it so I couldn't sing along.

We finally decided to take a long time off from touring and start recording our second album. I broke up with the boy and wrote a bunch of songs about California, about how despite the fact that he'd come back to Iowa, that I'd actually lost him there in the neon burn of West Hollywood, in the dark corners where the opposite of fame waits patiently to attack. We used drum machines, told our family and friends that we were trying to push our sound, that this would be the album that really made people notice, the one that would land us a record deal. But we never got far enough to see if that would be the case.

One weekend in March I drove to Chicago to attend a wedding with a friend as her date. There was an open bar at the reception and, after so many weeks of drinking the cheapest thing possible on tour, it was nice to marinate my internal organs in Kettle One and Knob Creek. I drunkenly danced with a woman who had taught the bride's high school art class. I stepped on her feet, told her that she was beautiful so many times that I almost gave myself an erection.

"What do you want to do?" she finally asked me. "What are you all about?"

"I'm a writer," I said.

"What kind of writer?" she asked.

It seemed like a good question. I probably should have said a songwriter, but I didn't. I could have said a fiction writer, but the stories crammed onto my hard drive were all first drafts and half-baked ideas, things that I didn't think deserved to be called stories. I almost started to cry, but instead I just said, "I don't know."

I then went off about how I hated the Midwest, hated that there were no hot guys in Iowa, hated the small town where my mother had decided to make her new life.

I told her about my band, about how it left me unfulfilled, and how there was guilt in this, guilt for even considering abandoning the dream I shared with my band mates, people who I considered my siblings in the silence of my heart. I remember slurring the phrase: "My life is not my own." And then I told her what I hadn't told anyone else until then, that I'd applied for graduate schools in New York and that I'd been praying that it would work out.

"And I never pray," I said. "I went to Christian school growing up, but I hardly ever pray anymore, and all my prayers now start out with me apologizing to God for only talking to him when I want something."

She touched my face like she was going to kiss me, and I could see my date and the bride and some of the other girls this woman had taught in high school staring at us in shock, waiting for the scandalous moment where their gay friend and their forty-five-year-old former high school art teacher make out on the dance floor. Instead she just said, "Don't worry. Everything will be fine."

I drove back the next day with my head pounding from too much booze, but even the hangover felt bourgeois, not at all what happens when you drink from a tap in a bar labeled BAND BEER. I had the stereo off so I could listen to my own mind, and my inner voice kept asking where to go from here? At one point it told me to keep driving, to head out to LA and find the gay director who'd spent the previous summer trying to sleep with my boyfriend. I would tell him, "Make me famous or I'll kill you." And I would mean it.

I was probably an hour outside of Chicago when I saw a kid around my age waving from the side of the interstate next to a stranded Ford Taurus. I was approaching at seventy-five miles an hour, which didn't leave me much time to think, but before I knew it I'd pulled over and he was jogging up to my car. I didn't know exactly what I was doing. I'd never picked up a hitchhiker or anyone stranded by the side of the road before. The voice of reason always propelled me past these people when I saw them, told me the car behind me or the car behind the car behind me would stop and help. I think I stopped out of desperation, because I was the one who was stranded.

I don't remember his name or even really what he looked like. I do remember he had dark hair and during the trip to the next gas station he talked about golf and the Dave Matthews Band and how cool I was for stopping to help him out. He told me he was on his way to visit his girlfriend and hadn't noticed he was almost on empty because he'd placed a photograph of her on the instrument panel, the photo covering the gauge. He got a container of gas and I drove him back to his car. He thanked me and threw a twenty-dollar bill on the passenger seat before I could say anything, and soon I was back on the road heading toward Iowa.

He hadn't been out of the car for more than fifteen minutes when I got a call on my cell phone informing me that I'd been accepted to graduate school in New York. I remember hanging up the phone and going blank. I wasn't happy or sad, just sort of shocked. The scent of the hitchhiking boy was still in my car, the scent of someone who'd grown up in an overly air-conditioned house, the scent of someone whose mother sprayed the bathroom with something that was supposed to smell like lilacs but only smelled like chemicals. At first I thought that helping him made me get accepted in graduate school, but I knew that the world isn't that simple, and by the time I reached Iowa I decided that I was the reason I was moving to New York, that it was time to start accepting responsibility for the good things that happened to me instead of only accepting responsibility for the bad.

Leaving the band wasn't as hard as I thought it would be, and in retrospect I made the right decision. I still talk to my band mates, some more than others, and sometimes we talk about the things I've talked about here and laugh, talk about how foolish or crazy or perfect our time on the road was.

My life in New York isn't perfect, but I like it because it's mine and I made it with my own two hands. And as long as there's a future there is always a chance for failure, but somehow age has allowed me to push that thought out of my head.

I sold my amp and my guitar during one of those clichéd weeks of soul crushing poverty that almost everyone who moves to the city eventually encounters. I left the pawn shop feeling the way those teenage girls who throw their babies in the trash must feel. Happy and sick and practically frantic with the realization that you never turn out to be the person you think you'll be. Sometimes I'll pick up a guitar at a friend's place or at a party and see if I remember any of our old songs. Some come more easily than others, and if anyone asks what I'm playing I tell them it's something I just made up, just some chords that don't mean anything. There's no melody, no words; just a progression.

The thing that ties me most to the band is our music, the songs on my computer that I listen to when it's late and I'm drunk and I'm wondering if I made the right decision, wondering if I bailed too soon. Usually I think that yes, I made the right decision moving to New York and going to school and following my passion for writing, something I told my mother I wanted to do for a living since I was six. But there are some nights when I am certain that I was wrong, and all I do is wish the kid singing those songs was still alive. I wish he had had a chance to move to Hollywood and be on MTV and save a generation who believed in music more than anything else in the world, and on these nights I'd do anything to turn back time and do things differently. Or at least that's what I tell myself. But I can't mean it all that much because if I did, I never would have killed that kid in the first place.

THE 21ST MILE

by *Caitlin Dougherty*

A friend and I are spending the night in the "Forest of Cedars," also known as the "Forest of Monkeys." The guardian to the few shops on the road felt he needed to watch over us—two young girls, alone with just a tent, monkeys with very large teeth roaming the ground around us. He plies us with tea, stories in Arabic, and he continually shouts at us one of the few words that he knows in French: *Zero.* Our conversations go something like this:

Guardian: "Arabic Arabic Arabic Arabic *gendarme* Arabic Arabic *waa-waa* Arabic Arabic *compris?*"

Us: "*Non.*"

Guardian: "*Zero! Zero! Zero!*"

At which point he begins again. He gestures, gets up once in a while to really demonstrate, laughs at our non-comprehension, and takes a sip of his tea.

                                ◉

We all search for something; that something is usually the ephemeral feeling of happiness. This may take the form of an attractive and considerate boyfriend or girlfriend, *the* job, the best recipe for chocolate chip cookies, or that pair of black boots with enough heal to really show off your calves. Some people find their answers while others never really begin to question. I am not searching for many things: just a purpose in life and some kind of happiness. (A considerate boyfriend who does not give me pink roses would be nice as well.) Meanwhile, I feel adrift in a sea of successful people who seem to have the answers already discovered. I have friends who are fortunate enough to have chosen a direct path from the university to a job. They chose the linear path, whereas I took a different path. Some days, I wonder if I am chasing my tail.

I grew up in a small town in rural Montana. I had an older brother who set the golden standard for my family. He did well in high school, went to a good undergraduate university, and received his degree in aerospace engineering. Since graduating, he has received generous promotions and bought a house. He's getting married soon. All my life I placed similar expectations upon myself. But I began to wonder, is this it? Are these the only goals I can hope to accomplish?

Somewhere right around the time I was writing and hating my senior thesis, I began to wonder, who really cares about this stuff? I had spent so much time in my life stressing over grades and taking said information and committing it to memory for the next exam or essay that "real life" seemed to be as elusive as an albino monkey.

So I did what people do when seeking an epiphany: I joined the Peace Corps. Three weeks after graduating, I set off to travel to a country I had never known existed until I received a light-blue folder telling me all about Togo, West Africa. This was to be the setting for the next twenty-seven months of my life. I read the brochure that detailed life in Togo with increasing fear of the predicted cultural and emotional transitions. I understood little, but read each page with fat tears cascading down my cheeks. Togo is a country the size of West Virginia—I cried. There are forty-two local languages spoken—I cried. How to prepare for an incomprehensible lifestyle with only eighty pounds of luggage? At the time, it seemed like a poor math problem and not a veritable hurdle that must be jumped. When twelve bottles of saline solution, twenty of hand sanitizer, a two-year supply of tampons, three boxes of Ziploc bags, cooking spices, rechargeable batteries, collapsible speakers, and lotion went through the check-out at Target, it only mystified the check-out lady as much as it did myself. The first time I weighed the hunter-green duffle bag, I felt the tears again.

Josie, a good friend of mine, sat on my bed and said, "Caitlin, do you really need that Shakespeare book and the two anthologies of philosophy? Do you really need four bottles of the smelly hand soap? What about this construction paper? Why are you taking so much cinnamon? That's a lot of batteries. I think you've got too much. There is no way that is less than eighty pounds!"

Did I need or want this item? Would I use this in the twenty-seven months? Twenty-seven months and only twelve hours left in the States.

Coupled with my own innumerous contemplations, I had other people asking me questions like: "Will you have running water, electricity?" "What will be your mode of transportation?" "Will you come home?" "Are you scared?" I had no idea how to answer any of these questions. I could, however, tell them about the weird and potentially life-threatening diseases, snakes, and insects that thrived in Togo. I could tell them religious percentages, the name of the president, and the predominant local languages.

I did not know how to tell my friends and family how to communicate with me other than giving them the Peace Corps' office mailing address. How was I going to live without email? How was I going to live without—without my family, my friends, the English language, Altoids and Luna Bars, coffee shops, and my Sunday morning bagel with hazelnut cream cheese?

At the end of the three-month training, I arrived to face the most terrifying day of my life: alone in a courtyard, surrounded by well-meaning children and adults, animals, and ordered chaos without really understanding what the people were saying or why I was there at 10 a.m. on a Saturday morning. I was completely on my own for the first time since I had left my family in the States. No other member of my training group was there to translate or to share bewildered looks with me. I had completed French training and had studied a little in college, but I soon realized our trainers had spoken slowly enough for us to understand. I, however, did not understand a word of the diaphanous blend of French intertwined with Ewé, the predominant local language in that area. There were lots of gestures, while children put my bags on top of their heads. They then began sweeping my two-room house with water and a hard-stick broom, they opened the shutters and left me the keys, and then it was silent. They left as quickly as they came, and I still had no idea where to get my water, how to go to the bathroom, or even where any of these people lived. I could only sit down on the hospital cot that the Peace Corps had found, eat a package of M&Ms, and stare at a spider the size of my fist.

I remember going to bed that night too empty to even cry. And my mouth was on fire. My tongue, cheeks, and throat were literally burning. Earlier that day at the market, I had purchased what I thought was baking soda in order to make banana bread. Later, when I realized it did not have the same consistency of baking soda, I taste-tested it. I realize that the first rule in chemistry is to never taste-test a substance, but I still placed a few granules on my finger and put them to my tongue. Many months later, I found out that instead of getting *bicarbonate*, I had received *sud caustique*, or lye, a *very* strong base. I don't think I can emphasize that enough. For four days, I could eat nothing besides choking down a little bread and peanut butter. I could not even explain to my neighbors what was wrong, as they clucked in concern; I could only show them my red-ravaged tongue, all of us uncomprehending what the white girl had done to herself.

I went to Notsè, a town ninety kilometers north of the capital Lomé, serving as a small business development consultant tasked to aid business endeavors, improve basic business competency, and train members of the community. My main project was to start a citywide trash collection agency and develop a city-grid numbering system with collaboration from the local hospital, the Red Cross, and the mayor's office. Coming from the so-called developed world, it amazed me how much trash littered the streets and other public places. In the market next to where women sold their tomatoes, large heaps of trash sat in the midst of their tables, flies going between the tomatoes and trash. Children played on top of the trash heaps. It was not surprising then that each year so many deaths came from cholera, typhoid, and other diseases that could be stopped with proper waste management. I also helped build familial latrines to give families access to a toilet rather than using the outdoors. However, I do not want to give the impression that the Togolese are not clean.

They have strict lines between public and private space, and their private spaces were always free of garbage and well maintained. Togolese people take great pride in their dress, shower three times a day, and only use their left hands when dealing with unhygienic matter.

I never felt so miserable, ecstatic, depressed, or empty as I did during those two years. I grew up listening to the mantra that I could do anything if I just put my mind to it; however, I could not pave Notsè's streets; give every person medication when they fell sick; or really ameliorate their lives in any tangible way. I could only listen and give what I thought was good advice and try to teach others so that they could continue the cycle. I could never be a member of their culture. I filled the role of the stranger: always participating but never quite belonging. I never felt that I was doing enough or integrating myself fully. At the end of some days (or even at the start), I could not bring myself to walk outside my gate to continue the onslaught of Togolese life. I would sit inside, listen to BBC World Service or music, and read back issues of *The Economist*—anything to keep the reality of braying goats, staring children, French, and the hot searing sun away.

It was not easy to adjust to their culture. The first time I got into a bush taxi, I felt violated. There were people with masked faces and brightly colored clothing, tied-up goats, shrieking chickens, and four to a seat that was built for three. But then I grew to love bush taxi rides—the silence, the closeness of people, the ability to stare uninhibited, and watching mothers take joy in their children's softness. Each time I got in a bush taxi I vied for the position closest to the window so that not only could I get to control the airflow, but also so I could see the palm trees, the lush fields, and the stately baobabs. Women ambled with large basins of water or firewood atop their heads while children slept swaddled in African fabric on their backs. Corn and red chilies dried in large patches on the side of the road. A son perched himself on bicycle handles while his father slowly biked up a steep hill. Families and neighbors returned from the fields with hoes clipped on their backs, walking slowly with their recycled tire shoes. It gave me a chance to appreciate anew the Togolese lifestyle. Togo brimmed with life, a life lived outdoors and always social, and a life where strangers and friends were welcomed and greeted alike on a red-dirt road.

At the end of the day, the Togolese taught me much by their example: To learn how to greet everyone and really mean it; to give when you have too much; to share a meal together; to go out of your way to help another person; to smile and laugh more. They taught me to take myself less seriously and to enjoy life because it does not last long. They taught me that death is a part of life and a passing from suffering is cause to celebrate. I learned how to live with little and to reuse everything. Yes, I lived without running water and had to carry about seven buckets in from my well each day, but I started developing biceps. I was lucky that I had so much.

I learned to love Notsè one week at a time. I chased ducks on my bike, visited the same shop owners, drank the best soymilk every day, and learned to be a member of the community. In the first months, I tried to avoid the stares and the harassment that came from being a celebrity in a town of 35,000. In the end, I grew to like running on the national highway in order to hear people cheering me on as I came into town exhausted. I grew to love people stopping me on the street so that we could share salutations. I succeeded when I got the previously ill-tempered vegetable woman to grudgingly give me extra vegetables and smile at me each week. When a Nigerian businessman offered me a shot of green sweet tea after buying fabric, I then surprised him when I told him it was brewed from the second pot. I even grew to love the bratty boy who lived across from my house when he came with his wicked smile and crawled into my lap. In the beginning, I had a mental countdown of twenty-one more months left, and towards the end it turned into, "Oh my god, there are only three months left." It was time to leave too soon.

●

In Togo, I was immediately looked upon as a solution to any problem, as a talking and walking encyclopedia. I was asked so many questions that I could not even hope to answer one with enough certainty. At every gathering, I was placed with the notables of town, even though many of my Togolese counterparts did far more than I each day.

People sought me for money, visas, medication, counsel, or friendship. I was asked by random men after a five-minute meeting to be a second or third wife so that they could go to the States. I have never felt more out of my league than when trying to fill the expectations of the Togolese. The expectations were tangible, so vivid that with each meeting I felt I could reach out and grab them. I fell short each time. I never did enough. I could not speak French clear enough to give a cognizant explanation; I could not give everyone I met money or time; and some days, I could not even leave my house or answer the door when I heard someone clapping outside of it. *Stay inside*, I would tell myself, *pretend you are not here.* Some days I was not saving the village so much as I was hiding from it.

I was a young, white girl who was given a certain amount of automatic respect, but it took time to enter into the people's lives and earn their trust. During some meetings I stared at my calendar, vaguely listening to the French that surrounded me, putting on the I'm-really-listening look. At least I had stopped all of my colleagues from speaking Ewé during meetings. Sometimes my male colleagues took my ideas and then presented them to the mayor. Other times, they said something entirely different than what was previously decided upon. Out of respect for all egos involved, I fumed quietly, not wanting to shame them in front of the mayor.

However, one meeting was different. The mayor of Notsè, the president of the local Red Cross chapter, and a hospital worker all sat, pens poised, waiting for my pointers on the project. I paused. I saw what they viewed before them: a stranger, a young girl no less without a husband or children, who came in as a foreigner and thought she knew better. Then I spoke out. When I finished, the mayor cleared his throat.

"Is what she said actually going to work?" he asked. "Will this plan upset the other committee? Will it be finished in time?"

They accepted my proposal, not because they needed to humor me, but because they saw the logic and feasibility of my ideas.

But with small feats also comes larger frustrations. I have never felt so helpless when I, who had studied political science, could not speak out about the military coup that took place in February of 2005. President Eyadema, who had been in power for thirty-nine years after himself staging a coup, died on the fifth of February. I was at a party at another volunteer's house, sixty kilometers south of my post, when our cell phones began ringing. Some of the Togolese had been waiting thirty-nine years for President Eyadema to die. He had held onto power tenaciously with the help of his military and, some say, by paying off foreign dignitaries to look the other way. The Togolese had waited, prayed for change. Even when I first arrived, many Togolese asked me when President Bush would arrive to liberate their country; after all, he was doing that for Liberia, Iraq, and Afghanistan.

Not very long after he died, the RPT (the military's party) and Eyadema's behind-the-scenes colonels appointed Eyadema's son to be the new president, Faure Gnassigbe. They bypassed the constitution's law and strong-armed the members of parliament to vote yes. Most people knew that if they said no, they or members of their family would be found dead in a swamp outside of Lomé. The "international community," a.k.a. the African community and the European Union, reacted strongly and called for transparent elections to be held under Togo's constitutional law. Faure acquiesced, and elections were set for April 24.

From February to April, hope and elation were powerful. The Togolese talked more than ever during that time, to a point where it seemed like that was all that they did. Men talked politics under mango trees while playing cards during siesta. Newspaper ads, logos, and t-shirts with each person's chosen candidate began making their appearances. I lived in a fairly strong opposition region, and it was exciting to see so much passion from the Togolese. Exiled leaders returned from France to unite the country's opposition against RPT, Mr. Eyadema's political party, but to no avail. RPT won in almost every prefecture, even the staunchly held opposition prefectures. They won 110 percent of the vote in one.

I could not speak out after the election results were announced and the gendarmes dispelled tear gas and shot at the villagers, all because they were demonstrating against the lack of a transparent and fair election. I could not speak when an opposition member in Notsè was shot dead and his wife later tortured. I could not speak, but instead had to stay inside my house and listen to the gunshots from my porch. I could not speak because of security concerns and the Peace Corps' apolitical stance. All I could think was: *Do I stay or do I go? Do I speak out to let the world know what is happening in a country most have never acknowledged even exists? Do I stay, to make a marginal impact on a small town?* For ten days after the results, I stayed largely in my house as my once lively city became a ghost town. Houses closed their shutters and businesses kept their doors half open to allow only one customer in at a time. Prices of food skyrocketed and everyone began buying rice and tomato paste in case riots or worse happened again. Husbands talked of sending their wives and families to outlying villages. Trucks with military men wearing red berets paroled the streets with their machine guns pointed at the houses. Telephone lines were cut and cell-phone reception was only turned on for maybe a few minutes a day. My only source of news was from the BBC or Radio France International, and their hysterical reports of approaching civil war in Lomé, looted French homes, and the destruction of a German cultural center did not calm me down. I could taste fear in the silence.

The new president pledged to work with opposition leaders and the talks began. Stores started opening, and we had reliable landlines eighteen days after the results were announced. The national highway was reopened, and the military personnel left. I finally was able to send emails to concerned family members and friends. Red Cross local officials were told to stop reporting the number of deaths allegedly caused by the military torture a month after the election. Togo, to the media, had returned to normal.

•

I cannot explain how Africa got under my skin. I wonder when I will return again. I traveled from developed to developing world and back, lost my heart somewhere among the palm trees, and drank one too many cups of mint tea. I remember leaving the Madrid airport with hesitation to return to an American lifestyle of deadlines, stress, shopping malls, traffic, and keeping up with appearances. When I arrived at the Newark terminal, I was surprised that without effort I understood what was being said around me. Hours and connections later, my parents stood outside one of the two gates in the Missoula, Montana, airport, wearing cautious smiles and shiny eyes to pick up their daughter.

"You know, our daughter is the one in the red leather jacket, the bone necklace, those dangly earrings, and the wooden bracelets," they said to the rancher in the Carhartt jacket next to them, "She just got back from Africa."

"Africa, huh?"

Before Togo, life was composed of separate and individual parts, and at the end of life, these parts presumably could be strung out much like a kid's train track. This is where it started, and this is where it ended. Now, my life is something that neither defines nor inhibits me. There is more to it than stacking up accomplishments and awards to characterize, validate, and enrich myself. However, these thoughts come on the good days. On the bad days, bed is a warm escape, blocking out thoughts of failure, of loneliness, and of not achieving enough in the real sense of success versus failure. These are the days when the cookies are eaten, the romantic comedies are watched, and the escape into a book is needed. These are the days when I avoid myself.

Sitting in a house surrounded by a washing machine, running water, cable TV, and a stocked fridge, I miss Notsè. I miss Togo. I miss the children with their swollen bellies, bare feet, and shy smiles. I miss my laundry lady who came each week, and I miss her giggle when she knocked mangoes from my tree with a broomstick. I miss the smoky air saturated with the smell of rotting fruit, spices, fresh dirt, flowers, and even urine—a smell that only one who loves this region of Africa can miss. I miss *piment* (chilies), warm smiles, and picking up my mail on Friday mornings. I miss hearing the roosters crow at all hours of the day. I miss the chaos on the streets and in the market, the *"excuse?"* when someone came to say hello, and passing the time with my colleagues at the hospital. I miss the dull *thwap-thwap* sound at sunset when someone pounded *fufu*, a gelatinous mashed-potato type staple food served with a spicy sauce, as it would filter over the BBC on my radio. I miss negotiating prices for a handful of tomatoes with used Western clothing. I think of my friends still there, who took care of me, making sure my bike's tires had air or that I was in good health.

The unexplainable love and loss that grips your heart is difficult to convey to another person. I feel lost. I can neither believe that I lived my life there for two years nor that it is over. I feel that I will return at the end of the week so I may see my friends and go to Saturday's market again. At the market I will buy tomatoes, onions, cucumbers, peanut butter, soymilk, bananas, bread, eggs, and avocados if there are some. I will then check my email at the one Internet café in town, call my colleague so that we may have a Sunday night meeting, and visit Helen, an Amazonian woman who gives me the hardest hugs. I may even buy some of the African fabric, *pagne*, and take it to my tailor to be sewn into a new skirt.

It hurts that it may be a long time before I will be able to do this again, and I know it will never be the same.

People are curious about my life in Africa, but I have very few people near me who can really understand the life I was living. People ask decorous questions, but most only want the ten-second version, and I cannot sum up my life, my adventures, or my heartache in ten seconds. I may bring up a story that is funny to me concerning people I know in Togo, and I laugh to blank stares. I speak less of Togo now and stare at the mountains more. My *franglais* has dissolved from my vocabulary unless I have had too much red wine.

I see well-meaning people here in the States who ask me, "So what are you going to do now?" I want to reply, "I am going to live," but that reply is not in the sanctioned conversation book. Instead, I smile and mumble something about taking a break and figuring out my options. It was a lot easier when I had a title. I could tell people I was a student, a volunteer, or on summer break from college. Now I do not have that armor, but instead I have to avoid people until I can find my sound bite to shout at the world. It is better than telling people I want to write or take a salsa class in my spare time.

Am I lazy or crazy? I feel that someone stole my body and placed it here, but my head and heart got lost in transit. I am sure the UPS man will soon deliver my heart, wrapped in a neat, brown carton, bearing postmarks from Notsè, Marrakech, Paris, and Timbuktu. And then someone will email me my head with a message saying, "Wake up and find a job because you cannot continue this forever." Presently, I only sew the memories into my consciousness, stare at my pictures, listen to my "world" music, and try to make the two realities meld into one, the present one.

For now I feel content to go through the motions. I hate it as much as I know it is the only thing that I am capable of doing at this moment. I focus on the small things in life: crosswords, Suduko, chai in the morning, afternoon naps, letters received in the mail, and down pillows at night.

I have broken down more than once since returning home—whether I crawl into bed with my mother or sob quietly in my room. I hiccoughed to my mother the other night that I don't even know who or where I am. Where did that confident girl go that existed in Africa? Where is her laugh and casual manners? Even now, a couple of months since I have been home, I still feel that someone is going to wake me from this dream. Surely, I am not really here.

I'm twenty-four. I know that I have to find a job someday, and start thinking about retirement, investing in high-yield stocks, marriage, and children. I see wrinkles appearing above and between my eyes, gravity taking its toll, the width of my thighs, and slowing metabolism. I am too young for cocktail parties and polite conversation around a couples' dinner table, but I have left the college days behind of immature prattle, that was, like, oh-my-god, like, amazing.

When I think of where my mother was at my age, I hear an avalanche. She had not only been married for four years, but she also had my older brother in tow. My grandmother had been married for five years when she was my age. My mother keeps telling me that it was a different generation, but I have friends who are leaping. Still, I feel too young, too immature, and I can barely feed my dog (one night, I had to resort to giving him mangoes and rice). I cannot commit on that scale to anyone because I cannot even decide what movie I want to rent. Do I want a comedy, drama, or foreign film?

I am a woman (some days) who must somehow juggle a career, her dreams, the house, and a spouse, and who must have children before thirty-five because then, they say, the ovaries do not work quite as well. But before having children, I must find a good job and reach the top of the pay scale before taking paid maternity leave. Then I need to find a decent, crime-free neighborhood where the schools are good. I get exhausted even thinking about it.

I become bitter when I think that it is still the woman's job to be the nurturer, the romantic, and the one who folds the socks. Granted, I like doing laundry and being affectionate, but I also want to be nurtured. I want someone to tuck me in at night, to tell me a bedtime story, and to display my art pieces on the fridge. I also want to hold the hammer, wear the pants, and drive on the road trips because I will ask for directions, on occasion.

Forget about the future plan, for now my entire social life is a wreck. I am now the conversation stopper. I am that poor girl that everyone pities because she is so socially awkward. I went out the other night and even impressed myself that I could still apply makeup, much less double a lipstick with a gloss. The red shoes and my new favorite pair of jeans came out of the closet. But when it was time for everyone to share their "what does everyone do?" I almost ran to the bathroom. What do I say? Do I risk telling people that I am unemployed or that I just got back from Africa? Will they run thinking I have some strange disease? It is bad enough that I have forgotten how to act around other Americans without having to answer *that* question.

I should have lied and said that I was a dog walker. Everyone understands what being a dog walker entails. And I like dogs because they accept people so eagerly with a wag of their tail. My sharp-eared African dog is sometimes the only anchor I have to sanity. Instead, I told the smiling group of inquiring minds that I had recently returned from Africa.

(awkward pause)

"Oh, that's nice."

"Was it hot?"

A couple of days later at a local bar, I met a silver-haired man who flew planes in Libya. After awhile he began to introduce me to other people around the bar. Even though I could talk to him of corruption and paying people off with pens, he introduced me to a rancher type whose shaggy blonde hair placed him in my age range. After hearing I had recently returned from Africa, he politely excused himself.

*

Why do I have to be serious and career driven? If I decide to move to Hawaii and learn how to surf, why would people find joy in commenting that the former valedictorian is spending her days surfing? Success means different things to each person. Normally, people define success by material objects and assets. I do not object, per se, to this standard, I only demand, "Is there something more at the end of the day, at the end of a life?"

My dreams scare the hell out of me. I dream about the book I am to write—the creamy, crisp white pages broken with the slight indent of black type. I run my hand over the jacket and feel the smooth weight to it. I see my name in type. I smile, and then I break out in a sweat. This is something I hold to myself protectively, rarely telling anyone. I've also fantasized about becoming a doctor and working for Doctors Without Borders. Since being back in the States, I have begun a post-baccalaureate/pre-medical program after having a crisis of conscience; but what about the applications, the time commitment, and the years of schooling? I live in hesitation.

Somehow living and working in Togo gave me confidence to pursue goals I previously thought were out of my reach. Before the Peace Corps, I could run maybe two or three miles at most. I surprised myself one day in Togo when I ran nine. I had always wanted to run a marathon, but in that hazy, undefined way of also wanting to write a novel. A friend and I signed up for a marathon in France after I left Togo. Could we run the 26.2 miles? Neither of us would consider ourselves runners or even athletes, and yet we logged long runs each weekend and started skipping out on social events in order to wake up and run the next morning. On registration day, we marveled that the rest of the runners were composed largely of graying men wearing t-shirts from past races who looked like they sprinted a marathon four times a year. My friend was recovering from a tendon injury while my feet were ripped apart from a just-purchased pair of flip-flops. The race started in less than twelve hours.

After missing the last bus and train, we had to hitch a ride back to our hotel from a man in a silver BMW. We named him God, and he smelled of rich cologne. During polite conversation, I told God (this was his twenty-second marathon) that I was planning on only running a half because otherwise I would have to walk the last part. (My training wasn't that consistent.) He said the French equivalent of "So what?" You run, then you walk. But you finish, and you cross that line. This is your first one, and you can do better next time. He gave us other pointers, and finally he dropped us off at a good pasta restaurant not far from our hotel. God saved our morale.

The next morning we ran with costumed men in drag and people running behind their own wine carts. We ran with people who stopped at each kilometer for their choice of red or white wine. I ran for hours, until my left leg cramped and my right knee ached, and then I walked. I crossed the finish line, exhausted and numb; I could hardly move my legs. But I had finished it. I had finished a marathon. Running had not really been the problem; it was the mental hurdles I hit at mile twenty-one. Now I need to prove to myself that I can do other things. I cannot wait until my mid-life crisis when I have more responsibilities and less time to have this same epiphany. I can make choices and live with the consequences. I can go from one day to the next. I am sure I will laugh, scream, cry, and suffer disappointment. But I have to leap, and with a little faith, my life will turn out okay.

I WAS A
WORLD-CLASS
DRUGGIE

by Vince Darcangelo

The front door grinds open with a lumbering scrape. Through it, two officers drag a ratty looking youth in mud-caked jeans and a grass-stained yellow sweatshirt. His head is bowed in semi-consciousness. The chains about his arms rustle as he stumbles into the admissions room and slumps into the corner. Each cop takes hold of an elbow.

"On your feet, Carter. Alright, turn around. Face the wall."

A burst of static and flange belches from a walkie-talkie. An officer releases the cuffs from Carter's wrists with a metallic snap.

"Turn around. Empty your pockets. Take a seat."

Carter slouches onto a green bench. Tangles of moppy black bangs snake through the arch of a backward-turned baseball cap. His face is a patchwork of uneven stubble, days-old dirt, and scabbed-over cuts. His eyes roll about the tiny white room, his jaw slack, his wiry neck barely capable of supporting his filthy head.

"Whose turn?" I ask.

"You're up, Darcangelo."

I search for an excuse not to take this admit, even consider making an appeal to trade down in the rotation, but the other counselors are busy with clients and paperwork. I begin to say something, then stop.

"You okay?" Jesseca asks.

I shrug my shoulders.

"I'll tell you later."

I pull Carter's file from a stack of recent discharges and browse through his stats. Once the cops leave I slide on a pair of latex gloves. Armed with a stethoscope and a sphygmomanometer—or blood pressure cuff for short—I enter the admit room and take the seat across from Carter.

"What's up?"

He gives a token nod.

I study Carter from the distance of a few short feet that spans three years. I search his face for recognition.

"Carter, it's me."

His pupils are pinned to half their size, exposing wet expanses of red-streaked white. Eventually, they twitch with remembrance. He blinks, rises in his seat, struggles for words.

"Dude," he finally musters.

He extends a greasy hand. I take it.

"How've you been?"

"Well, I'm in detox," he laughs with a slight cough. "I've started doing heroin since I saw you last. That probably wasn't the best idea, huh?"

We both laugh.

"The fuck are *you* doing here?" he asks.

A fair question.

I shrug my shoulders, smile.

"This is what I do now. I'm a drug counselor. How about that?"

Carter shakes his head.

"Too much, dude."

"Tell me about it."

I chuckle, then fall silent. I catch his eyes, hoping to peer behind that listless narcotic gape.

"We cool?"

He nods, then pulls up the sleeve of his sweatshirt and lays his exposed arm across the table beside us. His skin is a constellation of pinpricks; thankfully, none of them appear to be infected. I slide the blood pressure cuff over top his needle tracks, pull the Velcro tight, and pump it full of air.

I press the stethoscope to his skin and search for a heartbeat.

At twenty-six, I was a world-class druggie. There wasn't a chemical category or a means of administration with which I was unfamiliar, with the exception of needle injection. I had contracted alcohol poisoning; ingested LSD to the point of near-psychotic paranoia; done bong hits with the deputy sheriff; purchased bottles of Tylenol-3 from a crackhead in a biker bar (who was also selling Nintendo videogames from a plastic grocery bag); and had passed out at a Grateful Dead show from a toxic cocktail of sedative/hypnotics, goo-balls, Miller High Life, a devastating migraine, and a thick slice of French-bread pizza bought from an emaciated hippie in a brown fucking van. I had read Castaneda, Burroughs, Huxley, and Thompson. When it came to drugs, I knew what I was doing.

But for all my experience, I always sucked at doing cocaine. One night in particular was no exception.

Residue from the last three rails had collected in my sinuses and coalesced into a sticky, swelling snot-wad of Colombia's finest. Eventually it melted, and with one sinus-clearing inhale it slid down my nasal cavity and dissolved into my bloodstream.

Will was fidgeting spastically in the passenger seat, his lips flapping like automatic weaponry, as usual. An airy lisp distorted his stream-of-conscious ramblings. I was in my own vortex of intoxication, shoulder to the wheel, determined to get us to Jameson's house—where cans of nitrous oxide and a fresh pack of balloons awaited us.

But something happened on the way to the La-La Land of self-induced oxygen deprivation.

"Dude, did you hear that?"

I swear to god, my heart had exploded.

My pulse was throbbing in my ears. It marked a frenetic cardio cadence, keeping a higher tempo than the punk-ska fusion of Buck-o-Nine's "Nineteen" blaring from the tape deck. But more disconcerting than the breakneck rhythm of my pulse was one colossal leap of my heart like the kick pedal of a bass drum, thumping wet and hollow. It hit like a brass-knuckle shot to the ribs.

"Something's wrong," I said, twitching hideously.

Will continued his tangential oratory, oblivious. I pressed a palm to my chest, feeling for the next beat of my heart.

Thankfully, it came.

"Dude, my heart ain't working right," I said, a slight tremble in my voice.

Will raised a calming hand, pressed it to my elbow.

"Don't worry about it, dude. You're fine."

Will spoke with a tranquil certainty that put me at ease. I waited on his next words, ready to be convinced that everything was indeed fine. Will's head swayed, lazily scanning the horizon. He snorted, then finished his thought.

"That's just the cocaine hitting your heart, dude. It's all good."

I paused for a moment, trying to reconcile the seemingly contradictory phrases of cocaine "hitting" my heart and this being "all good."

"But isn't that a bad thing?" I protested. "I mean, my heart just popped in my fucking chest. That can't be right."

"That's just how it goes."

Will was nonchalant. He offered me a glazed smile and casually nodded his stubby chin as if I did nothing more than boot a ground ball in little league and he was giving me a pep talk afterward.

"Don't worry," he said, "you'll get used to it."

"Get used to it?"

I turned off of Foothills Parkway at the Valmont Street exit, two blocks from Jameson's house. We wound through a quiet neighborhood of townhouses and Volvos and pulled up to the curb. I killed the ignition, but retained my white-knuckle grip on the wheel.

"You're really freaked out about this," Will said.

"No shit. What should I do?"

Will waved off my question and repeated his calming mantra.

"Relax dude, you'll be fine."

Oddly enough, Will was right.

●

I walked into Jameson's feeling ridiculous. I should have, because I looked ridiculous. I was going through my baggy-pants phase, and my favorite was a pair of thin, olive-green plaid genie pants with a stretch waist and the density of a handkerchief. People couldn't tell if I was a hippie or an aesthete of thrift-store fashion. I was going for the latter. I'd bought the pants for $3 at The Salvation Army, and I wore them at least four days a week. They were really cool pants, actually, but they were about as durable as this shitty apron I once made in Home Ec class. Within three months they had ripped from overuse, sporting unseemly holes in the knees, thighs, and hem, and by eight months an ever-expanding gap exposed my right butt cheek.

In tandem with my decrepit genie pants I sported a black T bearing the likeness of Charles Manson superimposed over the *Charlie's Angels* logo, inserting the names of the Manson girls—Squeaky Fromme, Susan Denise Atkins, and Leslie Van Houten—in place of Jill, Sabrina, and Kelly. The shirt had grown tight from too many wash cycles, and my burgeoning beer gut was poking out the bottom. My hair was half-purple then, spiked at stiff angles that accentuated my quickly receding hairline. To top off the ensemble, I wore a green corduroy jacket two sizes too big and sat on Jameson's couch with my arms defiantly crossed.

Next to me was Julie, a dirty blonde riot grrl from New York. Her accent was imperceptible until the introduction of intoxicants to her system, then her voice drawled and soared with righteous East Coast rage and often got us thrown out of bars. On the coffee table before her sat a row of gray nitrous oxide cans lined up like bullet shells, and a pile of spent balloons. When it was her turn to fry, Julie would pick up each canister and shake it, searching for one that wasn't drained. She was babbling about something, but her thick Brooklyn accent was all I could discern.

Only Jameson, sitting across from us in an easy chair—looking J. Crew, like always—could understand her. That made sense, since half the nitrous cans were his. He attentively followed Julie's every train of thought and laughed at what seemed to be the appropriate times, but after all, who was I to judge what was appropriate? At first I wished for subtitles to their hilarious, gassed-up conversation. Then I thought, not so much.

Flanking Jameson were Carter and Stoney, two would-be bangers—baggy FUBU jeans and tilted ball caps in tow—who were snorting rails with Will. Carter's smile was wide and devilish, almost sarcastic—"Life is hard, but I'm harder," his smile seemed to say. His toothy grin could melt hearts and kickstart a rumble in equally short measure. Then Stoney lifted his head from a line of fresh powder, squinted his eyes, and launched into a lecture on the dangers of nitrous.

"You people are idiots. That shit is terrible for you."

As cokeheads, Carter and Stoney had major philosophical differences with the huffers, Jameson and Julie, even though the two Js could do blow with the best of them. But as the pile of powder on the table grew smaller, tongues became looser, anxiety tighter. A violent tension gripped the room, as it so often did in those days. We didn't know what was coming, but it was bound to involve fists.

Then Jameson sucked down a monster-size balloon and fell to the floor laughing, thus kicking off one of the most absurd exchanges in the history of recorded drug use:

Stoney: (to Jameson) "Dude, that's messed up. I can't believe you're putting that nitrous shit into your body."

Carter: (taking a seat next to Julie on the couch, stroking her hair) "Seriously, honey, I can't watch you do this to yourself. I'll give you the rest of my 8-ball if you'll throw that garbage out right now."

Jameson: (to Carter and Stoney, between gasps of oxygen-deprived laughter) "Dude...what are you...guys talking about? Look at...at all that...you just put up your nose, man."

Julie: (laughs maniacally)

Me: (arms crossed, look of terror, saying nothing)

The source of contention between the cokeheads and the huffers is that cocaine is an extroverted body buzz while gas is an introverted head trip. Cokeheads can't understand why the huffers want to check out when there's so much to do; huffers can't understand why the cokeheads are running around like mad when there's so much to think about. Both groups feel that the other is wasting a perfectly good high.

Stoney: (to Jameson) "That shit is killing your brain cells. They don't come back, you know. You're making yourself stupid huffing that crap."

Carter: (to Julie) "You're so pretty. You know that? You're so pretty, you don't need to use that shit. You're beautiful."

Jameson: "You can't...be serious...(gasp). You can't..."

Julie: (laughs maniacally)

Me:...

•

Strange as it seems, the cokeheads were right. Nitrous is bad news—and certainly more damaging long term than cocaine. But huffing nitrous oxide is also a lot of fun. Under the circumstances, I had to side with the huffers. I would have voiced my defense if I could, but the residue of drugs and panic had paralyzed me. I was just about sober at this point, but thoroughly defeated and barely capable of rising from the couch.

Regardless of who was right, it came down to one thing: Who the hell is going to listen to a roomful of coke-heads—powdery snot still dripping from their nostrils—lecture about what constitutes dangerous drugs? At one point Jameson became functional enough to call Stoney out on his cocaine use. Stoney responded, "This shit will kill me, but it won't make me stupid. It won't kill my brain cells. Nitrous will make you a vegetable. I'd rather be dead than stupid."

He was serious.

Ultimately, Will was able to keep the peace, rising from his chair and calling off his boys. Somebody cranked up the Beastie Boys' *Hello Nasty* on the stereo and everybody did their drug of choice, got wasted, and we all lived to get high another day.

Sort of.

I'd done the worst thing I could have possibly done under the circumstances: I'd sobered up. I didn't inhale any of the nitrous, and I certainly didn't touch another granule of cocaine—ever again. I drank one beer to calm my nerves, and that's it. It seemed to be a sensible course of action, considering my earlier scare. What made sobering up such a bad idea was that I had had to endure the inanity of the "Great Cokehead/Huffer Debate of 1998" with full faculties. Oh, god, how I wanted to leave, but was still too panicked to get behind the wheel of my truck. I stayed on the couch, as if in a coma, while a one act of hard drug theater delivered an overdose of pathology.

Stoney: (to Jameson) "Damn, dude. Did you...did you see what this motherfucker just.... Damn, dog."

Carter: (to Julie) "Do you want to hang out sometime? Stoney and I, we've got a band. You should come hear us practice sometime."

Jameson: "Dude, you...(gasp)...you're so like.... Ha!"

Julie: (laughs maniacally)

Me:...

•

A little while later, Will packed up what was left of his stash and we left.

"You alright?" he asked as I slid behind the wheel.

I nodded—obviously lying. But I was actually doing better than you might think. At least that's how I remember it. For all that had gone wrong that night, I was now aware of slight changes in my brain chemistry. My dopamine levels had receded to normal, and, in the wake of the chemical rush, the wiring in my brain had been altered—in a good way. I knew at that moment that my heavy drug using days were over. I said as much to Will as we headed back toward the highway. He scoffed at this declaration. He had heard this sort of statement many times before from his other drug buddies.

But he had never heard this from me.

"I'm serious. I'm done."

"Dude, you'll be back on the train tomorrow," he said.

This time Will was wrong.

•

For me, drugs were not only fun, they were also tools of socialization. They were a source of instant camaraderie, an excellent topic of conversation. You weren't just buying an 8-ball, you were investing in a built-in social network. I realized early in my friendships with Will and Jameson that they were chemical in nature. We were either talking about how messed up we were going to get

("Dude, I'm gonna get so wasted tonight"); getting messed up ("Dude, I'm so wasted right now"); or recovering from getting messed up and reliving the action ("Dude, did you see me last night? I was so wasted. And you.... Oh, man"). My identity was primarily grounded on feats of chemical experimentation, friendships with liquid foundations, and drug- and drama-laden sexual relationships with totally mental women for whom drugs were quite possibly the least of their problems.

But then, at twenty-six, I was suddenly a *former* world-class druggie. After that night at Jameson's, I was reduced to a beer drinker who would digest a reasonable amount of psilocybin mushrooms on occasion. That's it.

But still I tried to hang with my old crew—unsuccessfully.

A few months after the incident at Jameson's I was supposed to meet Will at a downtown nightclub, a place where we used to eat Ecstasy like it was Pez. I didn't show. It was the first and only time I've ever intentionally stood somebody up. It wasn't that I wanted to get back at Will for anything, it was that my stress levels were too high. Will wasn't an easy guy to hang out with. He often got into drunken fistfights, which meant you were ostensibly involved in some capacity. On one coke-fueled evening, Will got into a fight with his best friend/roommate over, of course, a girl and the fact that the roommate was moving out. But rather than duking it out, Will went after his best friend with a knife.

That wasn't the period on that era of my life. That was the goddamn exclamation point.

On the night I stood Will up, I had just finished a hella-cious double shift waiting tables, was tired and broke, and just the thought of having to follow Will into that abyss one more time pushed me to the brink of a breakdown. So when my roommate asked me to have a few casual beers at an out-of-the-way neighborhood bar instead, I went ahead with the better offer.

I returned home to find two messages on my answering machine.

"Darcangelo, where the fuck are you at? I've been down here an hour..."

I couldn't make out the next line over the thump of house music in the background. Then Will's voice returned with renewed ferocity.

"Show me some fucking respect. You'd better get your ass down here..."

His voice trailed off, then the phone slammed with a loud crash.

Will was more intoxicated, and more enraged, on the next message.

"Hey, fucker. You wanna play games? We're gonna play a game the next time I see you, bitch."

He finished with a drunken diatribe of threats, then slammed the receiver multiple times before finally hanging up.

I pressed erase and went to bed.

A month later, Will and I met up to drink some whiskey at a downtown bar. I was hitting on the bartender, Will was hitting on my friend. My friend was drunk, the bartender sober, so Will fared better than I. The three of us knocked back Jim Beam until closing, laughing through the final round. It was one of maybe five fun nights I spent with Will after that night at Jameson's. Inevitably, we broke contact. I lost touch not only with Will, but also with Carter, Stoney, and most of my other drug buddies as well. Some of the transitions were smooth. Most were not.

A rogue's gallery of girlfriends/drug buddies suddenly found me very unappealing when I became semi-sober. Eventually, they all gave me the boot. I don't blame them.

I would have hated me, too. I was dreadfully boring. I had no idea how to act, how to have fun. I became too serious, too uptight. There was something lodged deep up in my ass, and even I couldn't figure out what it was. Complicating the issue was that I was pushing twenty-seven, staring down thirty like an oncoming train. One score and six years and I was merely a waiter—and now a mostly sober one at that. I was lacking any career prospects, suffering from debilitating identity confusion, and tail spinning into an epic depression.

To pull myself out of this nosedive, I decided to try my luck with the straight community and asked a cute non-using girl to go with me to The Haunted Castle.

Afterward, Jesseca, a junior at the University of Colorado, was still laughing at me for taking her to a haunted house, both of us equal parts disappointed and amused by the cheesy nature of the Halloween attraction.

"So how's the fall semester going?" I asked, changing the subject away from my shortcomings as a date planner.

"Eh, my classes aren't so hot, but Vinnie, I'm loving my internship," she said. "I'm working at the detox."

"Wait, Boulder has a detox? No shit. What do you do?"

She said she was counseling drug- and alcohol-abusing clients—some working toward sobriety, some not, most of them homeless. She served as a part-time nurse and full-time therapist, caring for the drunks, treatment planning the sober, and leading them all in group therapy. There were chart notes, clinical meetings. There were people with degrees, with legitimate jobs—no, not jobs, *careers!* There were no nametags, no aprons, no add-on goals, no forced singing of dehumanizing birthday songs. Best of all, the entire operation revolved around alcohol and drugs. They were sober people, yet they were still speaking a language I understood.

"I've been training for that job my whole life," I joked. "I've been getting fucked up and counseling fucked-up people forever. I never knew it was a marketable skill."

Jesseca laughed.

"Well, you know, they're always looking for more help down there."

"You mean like—"

"Volunteers."

After a brief training session, featuring a crash course in first aid, pharmaceutical medications, and learning how to use (and pronounce) the sphygmomanometer, I was set for the world of recovery. Before long, my volunteer gig turned into a part-time job, and eventually a supervisory position.

I'm in my second year of life as a drug counselor when the inevitable happens: Two officers drag Carter into detox, and I'm forced to confront an alternate reality.

●

"Vitals are normal," I say, recording Carter's pulse and blood pressure in his chart. "Your body is holding up alright."

"Am I gonna make it, Doc?" he laughs.

His smile is the only tangible link between the Carter I knew and the admit sitting before me. It's the window to the self-destructive bent lurking beneath a good heart and an otherwise functioning brain. His skin has grown sallow, his features hard, his body brittle, but that smile persists.

"So, what do you want to do?"

Carter slouches and crosses his arms.

"I think I'd like to go to bed," he says.

"And then?"

He shrugs his shoulders.

"You know, I still talk to Will and Stoney."

"How are they doing?" I ask.

He shrugs his shoulders again.

"You know."

"Yeah."

I close his file and rise from my chair. I extend a hand. Carter takes it, and I help him to his feet.

"Want me to tell them you say hey?"

"Please do," I answer, then turn toward the drunk tank. "Follow me."

We walk down a long stretch of hallway toward a darkened room of plastic mattresses and busted Army cots. Half of the beds are filled with half-broken bodies reeking of alcohol, days-old sweat, and dirty feet. I lead Carter through the shadows to a corner cot. He slides into it and folds his body beneath the blanket. I search his face once more for that smile, that link to our former lives. It's too dark to see, but I know it's there.

NON-BABE IN

PORNLAND

by *Joshua M. Bernstein*

When I was twenty-two, I probably made you horny: I wrote tales of double-penetrated teens, slutty moms, and homely Midwestern girls spreading their legs like they contained the Atlantic Ocean. I was a written-smut editor, and an unlikely pornographer at that.

Yeah, yeah, I watched Skinemax flicks and slipped strippers the occasional buck, an all-American horndog. Post-college, however, I aspired toward fully-clothed journalism. Like many misguided sheep, I moved to New York City. I was certain that my headline-writing skills, which included community newspaper gems like, "100 Year Old Still Flying Friendly Skies" and "Where's the Beef? Back on America's Dinner Table," would net me a position at *The New York Times*.

Though I wasn't properly diagnosed, I was sick with the disease afflicting countless twentysomethings: entitlement. In this go-go, instant-gratification era, we want careers our way, right away, the easy way. I never fetched coffee as an intern. But my mama told me I was talented, as did teachers at my Midwestern college, which would *surely* impress every NYC editor. Harvard? Ha! I was an Ohio University alumnus. I merely needed to bide my minutes until a plum writing position plopped into my lap, like a golden egg from a goose's ass. It took three months to realize my aspirations were as unlikely as that magically shelled yolk.

Journalism was proving more difficult to break into than Fort Knox. Needing bucks—to afford more than a gummy-noodle diet—I took a gig as a human sign at Gucci's flagship store. The alterations room had moved a floor, so my duty was standing mannequin-still and saying, "The alterations room is downstairs." After two aching-calf days, I was desperate to quit.

Over drinks the second evening, a friend mentioned that the porn publishing company where she proofread was hiring. "You're perfect," she said, a statement that was either a compliment or character criticism. Weighing my morals against my three-digit bank balance, I scheduled an interview. After a brief chat with the publisher, the gist of which was: "When can you start?" "Next week."

I found myself working in the third floor of a fluorescent-lit Chinatown office building. While vendors outside sold knockoff Burberry purses and greasy lo mein, I sat in an antiseptic office ideal for dentists. There were no promo posters from *Backdoor Beauties*, pics of surgically busty women, or, especially, family photos. Makes sense, I suppose: Who wants their second-grade son's face next to a copy of *Naughty Neighbors*?

My company's porn-ladder rank was bottom rung. We published two magazines: *Cuddles* offered naïve, visibly uncomfortable white teens, while *Hot Chocolate* was its ebony sister. It sold very well in the Netherlands, I was told. Additionally, we printed nearly two-dozen, pocket-sized, newsprint digests filled with ribald stories and grainy images of women blowing bubbles with sperm like it was Bubble Yum. The prisoners, who made up the majority of our subscribers, loved these books best.

These newsprint-smudged tomes ranged from *Horny Housewives*, which explored faithless spouses trysting with pizza delivery men, to, sadly, *Family Taboo*: moms and dads and uncles ("kinky kinfolk," in the parlance) who explored relatives' orifices in such a nonchalant manner you'd think incest was an ingredient at every family reunion.

At my company I was, if you may, a jack of all jerk-offs. I reviewed cutting-edge smut, such as *Bootylicious Proper Hos*, interviewed D-list porn stars ("So what do you think of doggy-style?" was my favorite question), and, most important, pretended I was having sex. I scribbled the pull quotes accompanying every parted thigh. You know, like, "Pet my dirty kitty" and "I'm hungry—for your cock."

Laugh away, but this was an impressive imaginative feat. At the time, I was a shy, twenty-two-year-old boy with fewer sexual experiences than fingers. To me, crafting libido-arousing dialogue was like an untrained musician creating a Mozart-quality symphony. Or so I told myself as I segued into the second half of my job: the digests.

Filling twenty-three books with fresh, pants-tenting content every month was a formidable feat. Thankfully, I never had to spin a new story. A decade earlier my boss, a maternal Caribbean woman who loved hugging and calling me "sweetie" ("Sweetie," she'd say in her island lilt, pointing to a nineteen-year-old girl getting double-teamed on TV, "that girl can bend like Silly Putty."), bought a boatload of previously written porn. From amputee oral sex to anal escapades on a roller coaster, an article was available for every kink and quirk. So why was I needed?

This risqué avalanche was penned in the seventies. Back then, *Playboy* sold more than 7 million copies every month. America got its rocks off at the newsstand, instead of sitting in front of computers. Hence, lewd literature was in vogue, and writers cranked it out fast and furious. They wrote it quickly, sure, but well? Hardly. When a tale rambled, like the repairman arrived and examined the washing machine ("Oh, see, the D-bolt is not properly aligned—it's worn thin."), I sliced the prose until it was lean and mean. I also spiced up the more pedestrian yarns with my patented one-liners. You know, something classy like, "She swallowed enough cum to feed Luxembourg for a week."

I was a proud papa when scribing those lines, but one with a baby growing up far too fast. My company was stuck in the pulp-and-print past; the Internet sped forward, grabbing ever-larger slices of the tits-and-ass pie. We were shedding market share like a snake's skin, trying to attract new readers with impossibly erotic language.

"Make it dirtier," my boss would half-beg. She'd single out a single line such as, say, "Suck my nipples like a Bomb Pop," and implore me to make it world-beating, beat-off material, as if a few well-crafted printed words could stem the electronic tide. But the problem was, I couldn't make it sexier. After eight months of employment, my career reached skid-row levels: Initial excitement led to boredom before hitting rock-bottom depression. At each numbing shift's end, I hit happy hour like it was my second job.

"Another whiskey double?" my local bartender would say, pouring me the first stiff thing I felt all day.

Women were as thrilling as trigonometry. Eight hours of boobs and slashes of pink meant my libido took a siesta. Instead, I found refuge and love in a bottle. When a woman did chat me up, and I summoned the energy to be charming, the inevitable deal breaker was, "What do you do for a living?"

I would answer.

"Oh, well, I have to get going. Enjoy your drink."

And I did, night after night, until the World Trade Center tumbled down. My office sat ten blocks from the disaster. Every workday I smelled acrid air, saw the smoke cloud linger above the city. More than 3,000 people lost everything. I still had my life. Why waste it?

I didn't toil through college to peck out a career in peckers and pussies. Please. I was 900 kinds of overqualified—and underqualified in ways it took several girlfriends to understand. Smut was a stopgap, a delay tactic before barreling into real journalism, not just fantasies about super-horny teens.

Years, you understand, vanish with the ease of sugar swirled in hot tea. Youth is a priceless currency. And success achieved in your tender early twenties is worth double, triple, nay, quintuple that achieved in your third decade. What were my accomplishments? Temporarily curing a few inmates' loneliness, filling NYC bartenders' coffers? Porn was a slippery slope, dropping its merchants into an inescapable Black Hole of Calcutta that, to my ears, sounded just like an Indian anal-sex escapade.

I had stayed entirely too long at the fair. So, two weeks after the towers said a forced sayonara, I walked into my boss' office and quit, just like in the movies.

"It's not for me anymore," I explained, as I gathered pens, pencils, and papers, leaving XXX videos and magazines buried in my desk. Then I left the building and walked into Chinatown, into the ruined, hopeful city. I kept walking, faster and faster, until I got home, not even stopping to celebrate with a drink.

part:

3

RAISED IN
A ZOO

Zoo-raised gorilla moms often abandon their babies because they have never experienced another gorilla properly rearing a bambino. We are not *quite* gorillas, but people need some lessons too when it comes to raising kids, and yet children have such lofty expectations of their parents.

Some parents meet these expectations and are adored, with their children reminiscing about tree houses and teeter-totters, cupboards full of Ding Dongs and Doritos. While others slip into the unforeseeable—separation, divorce, extramarital affairs. A number of parental figures have a hard enough time slaying their own demons and can't provide everything a needy, desperate child craves, and for that they are scorned—rightly so, in some cases. But eventually we all learn that we have to let go of our childhoods, from the most blissful to the most horrendous, if we want to lead healthy adult lives.

Recognizing our parents as human is one marker on the adulthood yardstick. Paying our own bills is another.

How long are Mom and Dad required to pay for our car insurance? How long do we scrounge another couple hundred so we can make rent? Even if we *totally* need it, even if we feel like they owe it to us, even if they have an abundance of it, all that doesn't really matter. At the end of the day, we have to answer to the person who provides for us, and who wants to answer to their parents at twenty-seven? Along those same lines, how much longer is Mom compelled to take our 2 a.m. crisis calls? Is Dad forever obligated to say, "Don't worry, I'll take care of it?" We break away by inches—sometimes it's barely even noticeable—but it definitely takes some deliberate efforts on our part.

Then there's living at home again. Although it's often necessary in tough economic times, this is a hard place from which to blossom into our lovely adult selves, for obvious reasons. Mom feels like she can chastise us for smoking or coming home too late. Dad has us doing chores around the house again. Eventually, everyone starts to remember those annoying habits: the gum chewing, the after-dinner drinks, the shouting at the TV, the uttering of *like*. As soon as we realistically can, we just have to move on...and then we'll remember how much we actually all like each other.

LISTEN TO THE

SOUNDS OF THE HOUSE

by Jared Jacang Maher

When my father was young, one of his many chores was to spend a week shoveling three feet of livestock manure and hay that had built up on the barn floor during the freezing Indiana winter. It was responsibilities like this that had also built up the muscles in his massive shoulders and back, which today remain as one of the few physical indicators left of his rural tractors-and-church roots. Looking back, it was also probably one of the reasons why my dad would make me and my brother accompany him on semi-annual poop patrols through the neighborhood to recoup all that our dog had laid down over the seasons and reclaim it as our own. As boys we would follow him along the sidewalk armed with small shovels and plastic buckets lined with trash bags, scooping turds of all shapes and sizes, the petrafieds and the fresh-uns, from the manicured greenbelts and paths around our home. Inevitably, we would return with four times the crap that our Britney Spaniel mutt could produce in a year. For my father, the bags of other people's dog shit sitting at the bottom of our driveway at the end of the day symbolized a job well done. And that, in a small way, was social progress.

Of course, one man's utopian vision is another man's institutional oppression. My brother and I protested little during the years of fence-post-hole digging, tree-stump hacking, rock shoveling, sod laying, and the never-ending list of yard labor. At twenty-four, though, I liked to pretend that I was a grown man under no obligation for father-forced scutwork, especially those tasks of a stinky nature. But when back living with my parents, the past and future felt somehow locked in an unnatural embrace. It was like my new adult-self was on the couch making out with my old kid-self—and had everyone at the welcome home party feeling very, very uncomfortable.

One morning my dad came in from the garage wearing his leather work gloves and tattered weekend T-shirt, which had a minefield of little holes that pockmarked his torso. I was at the kitchen table, sitting in the same seat, in the exact same position as I held when I was twelve. The only difference was that I had traded Capt'n Crunch and the comics section for a mug of fair-trade Sumatran and *The New York Times*. My mother was out at various supermarkets, as per her customary five-hour routine of coupon-guided power shopping. I scratched at my stubble, reading an article on tort reform or something, while my dad consulted his to-do list on the dry-erase board mounted to the refrigerator. Today the list said: "mow lawn, put winter tires in attic, move cabinet, marinate chicken," and so on. Then, at the end was written, "show boys sprinkler drain." He asked me what my plans were for the day.

"Ahh," I drew out like I was in the middle of a really engrossing paragraph. "Ahh, I've got to, well, you know..." My voice trailed off. "Things like..."

My daughter, still in her Hello Kitty nightgown, poked her head up from the couch-cushion fort she had constructed in the living room. "Like what things?" she asked.

"Like important adult things," I answered. "Like giving-little-girls-showers things and brushing-the-tangles-out-of-their-hair things." Her head disappeared with a yelp. She knew that the longer I was left undisturbed with my coffee and newspaper, the longer she would remain immersed in a sea of warm, glorious Saturday morning cartoons. The program she was watching was about a group of grade schoolers who had discovered one of those little folded paper, fortune-teller contraptions, which they dubbed the "Cootie Catcher."

"Pick a color," one kid said.

"Red."

"Pick a number." Once the numeral was chosen, he worked his hands like little crab claws. "One, two, three, four."

"Will I get a new bike this summer?"

The little triangle flap was lifted. They gasped.

"Yes, definitely."

The whole story was about how the kids began to consult the Cootie Catcher on everything—if they should study for the next geography test, if they should swing at baseballs, if they should watch certain television shows— and how their reliance on its powers began to dominate their lives. Since they felt the future was pre-determined, or at least being shaped by some unseen force, they had no option but to hand over every decision to the judgment of the pocket oracle. But when the Cootie Catcher accidentally got put through the wash, the kids were left helpless, unable to function in a world of unrelenting choices and grand expectations. Were I to write an analytical English essay on the cartoon, I would conclude the Cootie Catcher was an indictment about the postmodern condition. Although I think my daughter thought it was just funny.

But I didn't need a Cootie Catcher to predict what my father had in mind for me that day. After I got Gianni showered and dressed, I followed him out around the side of the house where the manifolds for the sprinklers met the main water line. Eventually my brother crawled out from his bed in the pitch-black basement and emerged for the tutorial, only slightly more bleary-eyed and indifferent than usual. We stared into the hole while my father explained the system in wrenching detail. To drain the line between this and that, the uppermost valve here would have to be turned counterclockwise, etc. I nodded reflexively and concentrated on a very tan woman speed walking a stroller that contained a very terrified looking toddler. Both my brother and I knew full well that the process of draining the sprinkler system would be described to us verbatim again and again until the time came to actually drain the sprinkler system. That's when my dad would most likely fax us a meticulously written course of action and then talk us through the steps via a long-distance phone call.

In a month, my parents were moving to the island of Oahu in Hawaii. It was where my mom was born and raised, working in the pineapple canneries, and where my dad had fled for college as a way to escape the oppressively grey Midwestern sky. They were returning to Hawaii to work for the public school system—my mom as a special-ed teacher, my dad as a school social worker—while I presumably would hold down the house in Colorado until it could be put on the market and sold. I was unsure how I felt about the plan. My hope to get my own apartment somewhere downtown by the end of the summer would now be postponed for at least another year. The distance was only about ten miles, but to me it constituted a world of disparity. Even when we first moved into the house in my sixth-grade year, I had never felt quite at home in "The Ranch," a suburban hamlet named for the once pristine dry-grass prairie it plowed over for thirty-five acres of cookie-cutter suburban housing. No one in my family had golfed in their entire lives, a fact that would not change despite the eighteen-hole course that stretched through the development. For a time, we belonged to the country club at the top of the hill, which had a tennis bubble and pool. But somehow it didn't feel the same as the more modest, family oriented swim and tennis club we had left behind.

As I grew into my late teens, the distaste that I harbored for the place fit neatly into my budding political attitude. I scoffed at the preening elitism of the country-club members and their children, all dressed in cream-colored polo shirts, tooting toward the driving range in their electric golf carts. Every day around 10 a.m., just after the last SUV had rolled out toward the office or the mall, I would take note of the migration of lawn-care crews sputtering their battered Chevy trucks into the neighborhood, armed with weed whackers and leaf blowers. Despite passing two years of Spanish, I could string together nary a single sentence in *Espanola*. But as I trimmed the front-yard hedges in the blazing sun, I felt that somehow I shared a common language with my fellow landscapers. *Never give up, compadres, one day we will overcome*, I would think, brushing the grass clippings from my brow. *But for now, we must work...Viva la John Deere!*

The summer before my last year in high school, some buddies and I hijacked a high-powered golf cart from the clubhouse in the middle of the night and took it on a drunken joyride down the course. We declared ourselves revolutionaries and gleefully plowed through sand traps, small trees, and wetland bogs, stopping only to "plant" beer bottles into the green and urinate in the ball washers. When the police finally trapped our cart in a cul-de-sac, I was the only one who managed to escape arrest because of my thorough knowledge of the neighborhood's many escape routes, and my ability to climb fifty feet into a cottonwood tree and hide there until daybreak.

Four years of college and five years of parenthood had managed to tamper my tendency for beer-fueled vandalism and redirect it toward a penchant for wine-induced philosophizing. For me, suburbia represented the worst excesses of American-style consumerism. The endless sprawl pattern of soulless chain stores and outsized McMansions was a showcase of everything that was homogeneous, unsustainable, and wrong with the world. I had skateboarded through the multi-layered neighborhoods of New York and San Francisco. I had ridden the El train around every corner of Chicago. I had spent six months traversing Vancouver's bridges by bike. And now I was back to where I started, Westminster, Colorado, where my only choices for a bike destination was the Starbucks one mile to the east, or the Starbucks one mile to the west.

But more than the standardized scenery, I was increasingly agitated by the idea of living back at home. I had read the statistics about how more and more twentysomethings were residing with their parents, heard the varying explanations from social scientists who described the phenomenon as a kind of elongated childhood. Was it that young people had been pampered, they fretted, not taught the true value of a dollar and hard work? Yes, yes, that *must* be it. I wasn't as upset by this supposed generational occurrence as I was about the idea that I was a part of it. I hated the fact that I could be identified as a delegate in some pathetic cultural trend of leaches unable to survive in the real world, a cliché that has become fodder for sitcoms and local news telecasts. I had tried my whole life to choose a path of creativity rather than conformity, and here I was struggling to fit my identity into my old bedroom where I could hear my parents snore at night.

"Yeah, I'm staying out at my parents' house right now," I would reveal to friends and vague acquaintances. "But I'm, you know, just helping them out right now with some stuff. Yup, it is totally temporary." They would smile wanly and then change the subject. Because the truth of the matter was that with my random freelance writing gigs, there was no way I could afford to live on my own, at least not any kind of place where I could house my daughter during the three days a week she was in my care. In a practical sense, living at home was the best option for everybody. My parents loved having their sons and their grandkid in the house, and I needed a place to live.

But after more than a year at my parents' house, I began to ask myself, "Is any of this really temporary?"

One, two, three, four.

The answer is unclear. Try again later.

My dad was showing us how to replace a broken sprinkler head when an Audi with personalized plates that read "FLUFFI" pulled up to the stop sign.

"Hey, I see you still got those boys working for you!" yelled Jim, who lived down the street with his wife Cathy.

"Well, you know," my father ambled up to the car with the usual neighborly banter, "the only job they're really good at is cleaning out the refrigerator." Though he can be short and to-the-point when there's a task at hand, my father is not a harsh man. He laughs often and with great enthusiasm. It begins as a pained wheeze, with the growing hilarity stuck somewhere in his windpipe, building pressure like a Mount St. Helens of merriment.

When it finally does escape, the laughter explodes in a series of high-pitched shrieks. If seated at a dinner table, he will slap at the table with his open palm as if it has been bad. As kids, my brother and I would glance at each other wondering who this deranged man was, and how we were supposed to get him back to the shelter. Lacking a flat surface, he smacks his leg until the redness leaves his face, at which point he exhales and tries to recall what was so funny in the first place. He laughs the hardest at his own jokes. "That's just *toooo* much," he sighs.

"Well, we'll be sure to keep an eye on the boys when you're gone," Cathy beamed, and then called out to me and Adam, "No kegger parties now, alright you guys?" She laughed. "I have binoculars!"

I mustered a few ha-has and waved slightly. Adam didn't bother. For the rest of the sprinkler lesson, I made it a point to retain as little information as possible. After my brother left to go to work, my dad started telling me about how there was always the possibility that a winter cold snap could freeze a pipe, which could then break, flooding the basement.

"If you're upstairs, all you'll hear is water running," he said. "You know what that sounds like, right?"

"Are you asking me if I know what running water sounds like?"

"It's like a *wwssshhhh*."

"Yes, Dad, I know."

He said he knows I know, but then he took me inside the house and had me stand in the front hallway. He turned off the radio and told Gianni to go play outside.

"Listen," he said, pointing his finger into the air.

I listened. I heard a semi go by on the road. I heard a dog bark down the street. For a second I thought I heard an ice-cream truck, but it was just the neighbor's wind chimes.

"Do you hear that?" he said.

"Yes!" I said. "No. Hear what?"

"The house," he nodded. He explained that when one has been a homeowner for three decades like him, they become attuned to the noises their house makes. It's kind of like a residential mind-meld that creates a sixth sense for leaky faucets and dirty furnace filters. When my parents moved out of state, he said it was going to fall on me, this task of house therapy.

"I don't know," I said, half expecting him to pull a pebble from his pocket and order me to grab it from his upturned palm. "I mean, this house is so big. Do you really think I'm ready? Maybe I should start by listening to the coat closet."

I chuckled and waited for a reaction, but my father seemed lost in thought. He cocked his head and pointed his finger toward the ceiling. "That goddamn toilet upstairs is running again," he said, rushing into the garage for his tools.

In the first month after my parents had left for Hawaii, I felt like a new man. I began spending more time at home, amazed by its sudden emptiness. The pantry slowly emptied of the stockpile of Little Debbie snacks and cheese puffs that my mom would buy on sale, replaced with small plastic bags of dried fruits and wheat crackers that I would get from the health-food store. For my birthday that fall, my friends came over and we made fondue with a seventies-era melting pot that I discovered in the basement. Soon it was past midnight and we started taking shots of Jägermeister and dancing wildly in the living room to my mom's Hawaiian music CDs. I awoke at the break of dawn with a raging hangover and decided to climb through an upstairs window and onto the roof. The morning air was cold and there was a thin layer of frost on the wooden shingles. I watched the sun creep into the east, illuminating the long wisps of clouds that wrapped around the sky. Red, orange, yellow, blue. If someone asked me to pick a color, I don't think I would have been able to choose. The future seemed so distant and beautiful, but it was terrifying how all of it sat down on top of you, like a bully on your chest squishing your whole body until you couldn't breath. It was like the kind of freedom that's also confining in a way, the immensity of it all.

I stood and began making my way woozily back toward the window when I slipped on a patch of ice and started sliding on my ass sideways toward the edge of the roof. Propping my arm forward, I managed to wedge my arm against a skylight and halt my descent. When I got back inside, I took a shower, pulled the splinters out of my butt, and laughed, vowing never to die in such a pitiful manner. A jet-ski crash or a moped accident maybe, but never would my last memory be how the aluminum gutters needed to be dredged before I broke my neck in a bush that had become overgrown and required trimming.

I scored a job as a reporter for the local alternative newsweekly, and through the winter months found myself working excessively long hours in front of the computer and slogging through rush-hour traffic like all the other suckers in the 9-to-5 world. When springtime came I actually began taking pleasure in being able to be outside in the sun, away from my keyboard, doing something physical for a change. The first thing I did was water the garden, checking to see how the tomato and zucchini plants were coming in. I got the sprinkler system turned on again, but for some reason the water pressure was way too low and much of the lawn wasn't getting the proper moisture. For two weeks, the grass got hit with an intense heat spell and began to look brown and withered. Scared that the whole lawn was going to die and require re-sodding, I rechecked the manifolds and all the valves, kicking myself for not paying attention to the sprinkler lecture. Finally, I called Hawaii and my dad immediately identified the problem and all the steps to fix it. Soon the lawn was flourishing along with the shrubs and flowers.

After putting the mower away and hauling the bags of grass clippings to the end of the driveway, I cracked a beer and sat on my front porch. I admired how the lines ran parallel across the lawn, but rose and bended with the contours of the land, how the setting sun fell upon the straightness, the order of it all. Neighbors drove by and I waved cheerfully. I thought about my parents sitting in the middle of the vast Pacific Ocean. I wondered if they felt the same way as I did, returning to a place they lived when they were young—young, in their mid twenties, like me now—and having to reconfigure psychology with geography. The first house they bought together in the late seventies was a small postwar unit not too far from here. They both had full-time jobs and promising careers with health insurance and 401Ks. Eventually they saved up enough money to get a mortgage for a bigger house nearby. On weekends, my father built a huge back porch where we would have birthday parties and make homemade ice cream with neighbors. Where my father grew up, there was no backyard or golf course, just a huge cornfield and a long list of chores that had to be done if the family was to survive. When my parents decided to upgrade to the house in The Ranch, they did it for all the reasons anybody else did it—more square footage, better schools, the feeling of movement, change. If I were ever to buy property, this home probably wouldn't be my choice for a place to live. But while, for me, the house symbolized snobbery and conformity, for my father it represented hard work. And that, in a way, is progress.

One night I heard a car passing outside and I jumped out of bed to peek through a crack in the Venetian blinds.

A car full of teenagers had stopped at a house down the street. A week earlier someone had driven through my lawn and left tire-track scars deep in the Kentucky Bluegrass. I'd had fantasies of catching the punks in the act. Sometimes I smashed their windshield with a brick, other times I used the metal baseball bat that I'd begun to keep in the coat closet. But that night, the teenagers drove off and the night was once again silent. I checked on my daughter and pulled the sheets back over her slumbering body. I went downstairs and got a glass of water. I moved through the house wearing only my boxers. My bare feet felt good on the cold, hardwood floor. One, two, three, four, five, six. Is it possible to predict the future? *No, definitely not.* Instead there are only sounds. I listened to the refrigerator humming. I listened to the furnace clicking on and heat blowing through the basement ducts into different sections of the house, rattling the vent covers. But other than that, the house was quiet, and that meant everything was going to be okay.

MY FATHER'S
MID-LIFE CRISIS

In January, about a month before my brother, Den, and I figured out that my dad was having an affair, I decided to start seeing a therapist. I'd already been to see her a couple of times, and this evening, as I sat across from the petite, blond-haired woman, I could feel my body tighten. I tried to appear relaxed, though, resting on a bent forearm.

In past sessions, I'd talked about my home life fairly explicitly, as I didn't yet know about my father's affair. That only came up indirectly. I told my therapist about a couple of my past relationships and what it was like for me in graduate school. This time, I was determined to tell her about how I had been feeling as truthfully as possible. If there was something wrong with me, I wanted, no, *needed* to know.

Maybe it's just a trick of the therapist trade, but she didn't seem overly concerned about my anxiety and depression. I mean, she didn't seem to think I needed to be kept off the streets and away from small children.

While I talked to her, there was an underlying feeling of reassurance because I didn't have to keep it all in my head anymore. Just sitting there, though, talking out loud about it all scared me, too. It made it seem more real. My breathing felt shallow, and I was afraid to look at her.

"So," I continued, "I don't know what to do. Maybe I'll have to drop out of graduate school. Maybe I'll get a job as a library clerk or something. That'd be nice."

"That would be an interesting avenue to try. You like reading."

"I guess I won't be able to move out of my parents' house for awhile."

"No?"

"I just don't think I could be by myself right now. I don't know what I would have done without my family these past few weeks."

Then she said, "Hmm. Well, have you considered the idea that some, or a lot, of this could be due to living with your family again?" or something to that effect.

No. Yes. No, no.

I didn't know.

●

I woke up on the day before Christmas. Outside the sky was a crisp blue, as if it were the Fourth of July instead of Christmas. Hadn't it just snowed? I couldn't remember. It seemed like the sky had always been this color of blue.

I didn't change out of my flannel pajamas or shower. Instead, I made myself a cup of coffee and sat down at my desk. I'd been brimming with creativity for the past few weeks—it had started a couple weeks before the semester ended; I didn't know why. In fact, it felt like my imagination was on the outside, or maybe like my skin and tissue had worn thin and all the ideas whirling around in my unconscious no longer had any barrier. I felt very vulnerable.

I'd started my novel the summer before while doing an internship at a publishing company in New York. I'd never considered writing a novel before: That's like running a marathon, and who does that? "It's so cliché. Isn't every publishing intern working on her brilliant first novel?" I'd overheard a big-time magazine editor say. Really? Well, I could write a novel, too. Why not? So one Saturday afternoon I started writing.

Being in New York City was great. Everything had inspired me. All I'd wanted to do was walk around my apartment in vintage nighties, smoking cigarettes, and thinking, saying, writing inspired words. Being back in Boulder, Colorado—in my parents' basement, no less— was oppressive. All I wanted to do was work my ass off so in May I could graduate from my master's program not too heavily in debt and ready to go some place where things actually happened. What things? No idea. Fast things. Weird things. Glamorous things. New things.

Just as I was finishing my coffee and feeling a little dried up and tired, I started to run over in my head the list of things I needed to do that day. Neither my dad nor my mom wanted to cook this year, so I'd be going to Whole Foods to pick up the groceries for today and tomorrow. My brother, Den, who was named after our father, had already left for Massachusetts to work on the "Kucinich for President" campaign. I have an older sister too, but she and my dad never got along, so we never knew if she would spend the holidays with us. It was annoying that nobody seemed to care about the upcoming holiday but me. And I had to pick up a few movies, too. Then I'd have to hurry home and start chopping and boiling and dicing and baking and whipping and letting cool. I started to feel nervous...*really* nervous. Maybe as nervous as I ever had, and I didn't really know why.

I got in the shower and quickly got ready. I grabbed the pack of cigarettes I'd hidden in my sock drawer and headed out. Somehow I thought stopping off at the park and smoking a Marlboro Light would make me feel more at ease. It only made my heart beat even faster.

Whole Foods was a nightmare. It literally could have been a nightmare of swirling soup cans and falling walls: lost in a supermarket and surrounded by hundreds, thousands, of scurrying, more pointedly, angry shoppers. By the time I reached the cashier, I didn't think I could hide my beating heart and darting eyes and shaking hands. She rang up my groceries as if the world wasn't falling to pieces out of nowhere and for no reason.

How was I going to handle Blockbuster?

Once home, I started making dinner. My dad—who was born in England but mostly raised in America—moped into the kitchen to begrudgingly help me cook. I hadn't asked, but maybe he felt like he should. I didn't really care why he was there because I appreciated the help. My mom came down for a few minutes. The three of us were so funny and selfish, so wrapped up in our own emotions: Dad brooding, Mom only half present, and me trying to make everything okay again, everything inside of me and outside of me.

At one point my dad wandered off to check his email. A few minutes later, I heard my mom's loud voice from across the house, "Sweetheart? Is that email you're reading addressed to 'Sweetheart?'"

"No," was his muffled reply.

I started chopping faster.

My mother doesn't remember now that this incident ever even happened. I almost immediately forgot it, but then, when everything came out, I remembered.

That night, all I wanted to do was go to bed. Screw cake. Screw ice cream. Screw *Pirates of the Caribbean.* My heart hadn't stopped beating since I'd finished my coffee that morning, and I knew the only way I'd get any peace was if I was asleep.

⁕

Naturally, after I discovered the reason for my father's strange behavior, I wanted to talk about it with my therapist. I felt so angry and disgusted at first, and even though she didn't talk me out of those feelings, she encouraged me to see my dad, both my parents, as human.

"What happened?" I asked, one bleak February afternoon. "He's a good person. He always did as much as he could for us. Why did he stop caring about us?"

"Of course he still cares about you," she said.

"Maybe we were slowly draining him with all of our intense needs, financial, emotional, whatever else." Then I reconsidered, "But why couldn't he have just said no? For years and years, he never said no. Come to think of it, he still really hasn't. He just started *saying* one thing and *doing* another."

"Do you think," she began, "you and your father are possibly experiencing something similar right now, in terms of your fears? You don't have to forgive him—"

"I won't," I broke in.

"And you don't have to make excuses for him, because, after all, what he did was wrong. But are you able to see any of this from his point of view?"

⁕

Father woke up very early on Christmas to a near-empty home. In the twin bed next to him, his wife was still asleep. He quietly got out of bed and went downstairs. Yesterday his daughter had brought inside the small, potted evergreen tree they had bought the Christmas before, but no one had bothered to decorate it. After he'd spent a good part of the previous afternoon wrapping presents, he'd displayed the shiny gifts underneath the small, bare tree.

Father—now past fifty, with a receding hairline and bags under his eyes to prove it—sat down on the white-trimmed, blue couch and looked out at the still-dark street. He could see the high school his son and daughter had attended; the baseball field where his son had played; the track his daughter had run on. The street they drove on day after day, so familiar now, the same street on which they'd found the crumpled body of their missing family cat.

The sky began to turn pink from the rising sun, which was hidden from view by the walls of the house. The town-house had become somewhat reminiscent of the home he'd imagined for himself as an architecture student. He, of course, didn't design it himself; indeed, he now special-ized in designing prisons. But it was located at the base of the foothills, had a courtyard in front filled with trees and flowers and a red-tiled entryway that he'd put in place himself. When he was younger, he had imagined himself living in Europe. Now that seemed impossible.

He had recently bought the new Peter Maile—a best-selling travel writer—book at the local bookstore. He got up off the couch and walked over to the dining room table where he'd left the book the night before. Then he sat back down on the couch and started reading. Soon he heard his wife's footsteps on the carpeted stairs.

"Hi, Denys."

"Hello."

"It's Christmas."

He coughed.

"Should we get Bess up?" she asked.

"She'll come upstairs when she gets up."

"I don't like Den being gone." She walked into the kitchen and started to make coffee.

His son had a master's degree in aerospace engineering but had recently decided he didn't want to be an engineer. At twenty-six he still didn't know what he wanted to be, an English professor, a doctor, a political activist.

"Me neither."

"He only had a few weeks off from school anyway. I don't see why he had to give himself all these extra things to do."

"No. Well, at least he can spend Christmas with Uncle Louis."

"I'd rather he was spending Christmas with us. I'm sure he'd be happier here than there."

After a moment, he started reading again.

With her cup of coffee, his wife sat down on the oversized chair that matched the couch. The view from that seat was straight out. She looked a bit like a queen there. Drinking her coffee in hearty gulps, she watched the cars pass—though there weren't many that morning. Maybe it was the smell of coffee or the sound of voices or of footsteps that brought his daughter up the stairs and into the deflated Christmas celebration.

"Merry Christmas, honey," his wife said.

"Merry Christmas," his daughter's tired voice responded.

No one seemed all that excited when they took a seat around the little evergreen tree to open presents. And that year after presents, there were no blueberry pancakes.

•

On Christmas Day, after the requisite tearing open of and staring at glittering gifts, the house got pretty quiet. I had been downstairs sorting through some of the thoughts I had running through my mind. Not much sorting occurred. More running, actually. I walked into the living room. I sat down on the couch. I got up again. I walked into the kitchen. Then I went upstairs.

I found Mom sitting on her bed, her short, dark hair contrasted against the white walls of her bedroom. Italian-American, she had pretty olive skin and liquid brown eyes.

"Mom, I still can't relax," I fairly whined, as I climbed onto her bed and curled into a ball like a cat. "I don't know what's wrong with me."

"Oh, honey, I hate to see you like this."

"What's wrong with me?" I repeated.

"Nothing." Mom began patting my head, something I realized was infantilizing but in which I also found some relief. "You've been through so much these past few weeks."

"Yeah," I said, somewhat dubiously.

"You have. The end of the semester. No one likes the holidays...Peter."

"I guess it's over between Peter and me."

"Weren't you just saying that you were going to try being less demanding of your boyfriends this time?"

I sat up quickly.

"Mom, he never calls when he says he's going to call or does what he says he's going to do. He drinks too much. He's always either drunk or hungover. I'm not being too picky this time."

"No, no. You're right. I'm sorry. I was wrong."

"It's just way too stressful."

"Well, then, just break up with him."

"I'll just get it over with when he gets back from Christmas vacation...if he ever calls me again," I said.

"Good."

"I still feel really tense, Mom."

"You'll feel better when all this is over."

"Maybe."

"Why don't you go for a walk with your father?"

The word "father" had an aura around it. Just by it being said out loud, my mother and I seemed to relax a little, like some force greater than ourselves would now take over. And it was all going to be okay. Right?

•

Father was gazing steadily ahead as he and his daughter pulled off the state highway into the parking lot at the bottom of Bluebird Trail. He ventured a glance in her direction. She was staring out the window. Her hands folded in her lap. He carefully pulled into a parking spot, beginning to sense that something wasn't in order.

"I wish Den were home," she said, off-handedly, climbing out of the car.

"I do too," he replied quickly, with a little more vehemence than was customary for him. "I don't know why he had to leave now—at Christmas."

The two of them began walking along the muddy trail. It passed through a field where cows often grazed. A few cows blocked the path, and they walked off the path and around the cows. Just like the day before, the sky overhead was blue. The only sign of snow was the wet ground below them, wet because the sun melted last week's snow.

They were approaching a gate. Father lifted the latch and they walked through. Once they were on the other side of the gate, he secured the latch again. At that point, the trail started to climb, slowly rising up out of the meadow and into the foothills. They hadn't encountered any other walkers yet.

"So, I guess Mom probably told you about," she swallowed her words a little, "about how I've been feeling."

"No," he was solemn now. "What's the matter?"

"I don't know. I've been feeling really anxious the past few days, and I just can't relax."

"Oh. Is there anything in particular bothering you?"

"No. I mean, I think I was just probably so busy at the end of the semester and now that I don't have anything to do...you know, like I have all this energy but nothing to do."

"Well, you should use the break to slow down."

"I wish I could. But it's like I don't have any control over it, you know?"

"Sure." He coughed, looking ahead.

"Dad, when you were upset for awhile, you know, after you fell and broke your hip, what did you do to make yourself feel better?"

"Let's see. I tried not to think too much about anything. I read a lot. I watched movies. That sort of thing."

"Yeah, maybe I'll just read a lot over break."

"Well, I have a lot of travel books on the bookshelves downstairs. I always like reading those."

"Yeah."

Father had been staring straight ahead. Now he looked quickly at his daughter. Her face was flushed from the exercise. Her sneakered feet thudded against the trail. He could remember what she looked like as a little girl. She looked so much the same, he thought. Brown skin. Wide eyes. Skinny arms and legs. He felt his cell phone vibrate in his pocket. Someone was calling.

•

I got up on the day after Christmas. The sun crept in through the window. I felt warm, happy. For a moment. And then I started thinking about the fact that I felt warm and happy. Did I really? Had this phase passed?

No. The now familiar feeling of fear rose up from my stomach and spread through my limbs. Why get out of bed? Why face another day rinsed with dread? Why bother?

But I got up. I decided that today I'd get out of the house. I would force myself to spend winter break the way I had planned—drinking coffee downtown, writing, hiking, reading, spending time with Peter....

The night before Peter had left for Christmas, he and I had decided to go to Caffe Sole, a local coffee shop. After we'd been there awhile, Peter had gone to the bathroom and I'd slipped outside to smoke a cigarette. A young man and woman—maybe husband and wife—had stood next to me, very close, the woman smoking, too. Taking a step in the opposite direction from them, I'd begun to wonder where Peter was; I'd left a little note on the table telling him I was outside, but that had seemed like a long time ago. How long ago was it?

After looking inside and noticing Peter at our table again, I'd motioned for him to come outside. He'd asked, pushing open the glass door, if I'd been outside the whole time? He'd never seen the note and wondered where I was. Then Peter had laughed, indicating that he wasn't · really angry, or not anymore, and then, with a mock air of humility, said, "Can I have a cigarette?" I remember being glad that I had something to give him.

Walking upstairs to the kitchen, I tried to shake the thoughts from my head. I ate a bowl of cereal that tasted like cardboard and trudged back down the steps to my room. I didn't exactly feel like going out, but I had a plan. I would take the bus downtown with my laptop. I'd get some tea and sit outside somewhere and work on my novel.

My plan gave structure to the day, and I slipped myself inside that compartment. I showered and got ready, and soon was at the bus stop, on my way downtown, to a table with a cup of tea, staring at my computer.

I found that I had nothing to write. Besides, the other people around me demanded my attention. They talked so loudly. The whole café buzzed with the noise of a dozen or more conversations, all of which competed for supremacy.

I went to the bathroom for some quiet time. When I got back to the table, I packed up my laptop and left. I was headed for the bus stop where I'd catch a bus that would bring me back home again.

"Hi," I heard a woman's voice say.

After looking up to see the face of a creative writing professor at CU, I said, "Oh, hi," in response. Even though I was a literature student, she had let me sign up for her graduate fiction workshop in the spring. I had told her I'd wanted to work on my novel.

She smiled kindly and turned into the coffee shop; I walked to the bus stop, feeling sorry that I would let her down after she'd let me into her class.

Once home, I put my laptop and its case away and I tried to find something else to do. I wandered over to the bookshelf with the vague idea of finding a travel book to read.

I walked over to the part of the shelf that housed my father's books, but after reading the backs of a few books on Italy and France, I quickly became disinterested. Nothing about fixing up a home in Provence and meeting the local villagers interested me—but it was just the sort of thing my dad loved. I let my eyes wander through his other books: guide books, books on architecture, D.H. Lawrence, Graham Greene. I settled on Graham Greene's *Heart of the Matter*, a book, judging from the description on the light-blue back cover, about a man living and working in Africa.

But I didn't read. I didn't feel like it. I didn't really feel like doing anything. I wondered when Peter would call. Was he back from the mountains yet?

Father was making dinner; it was one of the last days of December. He made dinner almost every night. He chopped up carrots, peeled squash, boiled pasta, soaked beans, fried onions. Sometimes his daughter helped. Sometimes they ate leftovers. Usually, he cooked.

He also cleaned, he thought, while he tossed the red peppers into the frying pan. His wife did the dishes after dinner, but it was always he who cleaned the house on the weekends. Every Saturday. And he who balanced the checkbook. All the bills that poured in—for doctors and dentists and clothes and haircuts and dinners out. His pocket vibrated. Someone was calling.

Leaving the peppers frying on low heat, he ducked out the front door.

"Hello," he said quietly, as he walked quickly toward the garage.

"Hi, darling," a voice said back to him. He looked back toward the house and could see his daughter in the kitchen looking out at him.

"Hi, Rachel. It's so good to hear your voice. Can we see each other tonight?"

"Of course. I'm so happy that you're so happy to hear from me. I miss you."

"I miss you, too. Where should we meet?"

"Guess what?" she asked.

"What?"

"I think I've got a job lined up."

"That's great."

"I know. It's a contract job making promotional materials for a new wine shop opening up in Louisville."

"That's wonderful. We'll talk about it later. So, where should we meet?"

"Hmmm, where should we have dinner tonight?"

"How about Jax?" he suggested.

"We just went to Jax."

"How about the Med?"

"That sounds good."

"I'll see you at nine then."

"Okay, honey. See you then."

He quickly hung up the phone and dropped it in his pocket. He darted back to the house and continued making dinner. The pasta had probably been boiling for ten minutes, he figured. He poured it into the strainer and then turned off the stove top.

"Dinner's ready," he shouted.

His son—who was back from the East Coast—his daughter, his wife, and he sat around the table and started eating.

"The vegetables aren't cooked all the way, Dad," his son stated, lightheartedly.

"Yeah, they're pretty crunchy," his daughter jocularly agreed. "It's like you didn't even cook them at all."

Father grunted a response, and his son and daughter exchanged a look. He then announced that he was going to the pool.

●

After dinner, my mom went upstairs, and Den and I picked up our books and sat down in the living room to read. I was so glad to see him home. Where I was a realist, my brother was an optimist, and I needed a good dose of optimism.

"Dad loves that pool," I said.

"Yeah, it's weird."

He'd referred to it as his club, and I'd wondered if it reminded him of a time when he was a young boy and wealthy and living in exotic locales in big houses with servants. His parents eventually lost everything, and my own upbringing was nothing like his.

"Are you going out tonight?"

"Yeah, in about an hour. Are you going out?"

"No. I don't feel like it."

"Do you want to come with us?"

"Nah."

"How's Graham Greene?" he asked.

"Depressing."

"Which part are you at?"

"It's the part where he and his wife are at a party at the club, and he's miserable and doesn't want to be there, but he feels this sense of responsibility to his boss and his job and his community."

"Oh yeah." Den had read the book several months ago.

After we'd been reading for awhile, my brother got up to leave.

"You leaving?"

"Yep."

"'Kay, see you later," I said. "You sure you don't want to come?"

"Yeah."

"Okay."

"Have fun."

"Alright. Hey Bess, what are you doing for New Year's Eve?"

"I don't know yet."

"Yeah, me neither. Alright, see you later."

"Bye."

After Den left, I read for a little while longer. This poor man was trapped in a horrible world dictated by mindless social norms and heavy African weather. But the really sad part is that he could have handled it, but he had to take care of his wife too, and she hated the life they had more than he did. At the same time, I kept wondering why he couldn't just leave if it was really so bad for him.

I mean, if you're so unhappy, there has to be something you can do about it.

I went downstairs. Nine o'clock. Not too early to put my pajamas on. I was sure Peter was back from the mountains. Why hadn't he called?

On the night Peter and I'd gone to the coffee shop, I'd dropped him off at his apartment. I'd slowly pulled into a parking spot in front of his house. We'd sat there, silently, for a moment. Though we'd wished each other Merry Christmas, and he'd thanked me for the CD I'd made him, neither of us had committed to seeing each other again.

"See you later, dude," had been his goodbye. I'd smiled wanly, remembering how he'd told me another girlfriend hated it when he'd called her "dude."

Everything's going to be fine, I'd thought, driving away.

Since I already had my pajamas on, I figured I might as well get in bed. I thought about reading, but I was too tired and put the book down.

I didn't want to go to New York anymore, I thought, lying in bed. I wouldn't know anyone there except Cori and Marissa. I didn't have a job lined up, and I knew it'd take forever to find one. Besides, I didn't want to live in a city after all. Well, I didn't know. But right now it felt like it'd be too loud, too crowded, there'd be too many sirens and buildings and people and streets.

I didn't even know if I wanted to go back to school next semester. I'd signed up for that fiction workshop, but I hadn't written anything since Christmas Eve, and maybe I wanted to take a break from writing. The other classes I'd signed up for sounded too intense. Theory, heavy reading loads, long papers about the social construction of identity, and God knows what else. *Was* I just the product of my environment? If you stripped away the morals and values I grew up with, was there really nothing underneath?

If so, what happened when we died? Did we just rot in the ground? And if so, what was the point? Why go through all this pain and confusion and everything else just to die and have nothing come of it? And what about the people who were more miserable than I was? Bums, heroin addicts, sweatshop workers, people with horrible diseases.... Now my mind was racing, and I knew it'd be hours before I went to sleep. I remembered when the only rest I had was when I slept, and now I didn't even have that.

New Year's Eve had some sort of mystical significance for me that year, even if increasing feelings of hopelessness subdued that allure. My concrete New Year's resolution was to quit smoking. I'd been smoking on and off since I was seventeen, and now, at twenty-five, I'd quit once and for all. The vague idea was that I'd become a healthier, better person. Besides quitting smoking, it wasn't entirely clear how that was going to happen.

On New Year's Eve, I was going to go out for the first time since before Christmas. This was also somewhat momentous. It was to be dinner with my family at my parents' favorite restaurant—the only one, in fact, that they ever went to together—which was located inside a local hotel-resort, then drinks afterwards with some friends of mine from the English department.

I got a little dressed up and to a certain extent was looking forward to it. I wore a black button-down shirt with jeans and flats and the necklace my mom gave me for Christmas. I was nervous though. Prior to leaving, I sat on the edge of my bed and took some deep breaths. It was going to be okay.

When we got to the restaurant, we realized that they were refinishing the wood floors in the dining room, and so we had to sit in the lounge area instead. There were only a few other people in there besides us. One table over from us sat a man and a developmentally disabled girl who talked very loudly. Across the room sat an older couple. The odor from the wood stain leaked into the lounge, tainting the air with chemical fumes.

The waiter came over and we ordered glasses of wine and our dinner. I think the subject of politics came up fairly quickly: the war in Iraq, Bush's election theft, et cetera. I was sick of it and had nothing to say. My mother, maybe noticing my silence, asked what my plans were for that evening. I told her. I could smell the wood stain (it seemed to get stronger and stronger) and I could hear the other parties talking noisily. I took a sip of wine.

Throughout dinner, the wine made me feel a little more relaxed. It seemed to have the opposite effect on my father. At one point, he starting making faces in response to comments that the retarded girl made. At the first sour expression, Den and I exchanged a look. At the second, I started staring at my pasta, mortified.

When it came time to order dessert, Den and I opted to skip dessert and leave the restaurant altogether. We'd taken a separate car anyway so we could leave early and meet up with our friends. So we said goodbye and took off.

Outside, the air smelled fresh. I took a breath.

"Dang, that sucked," said Den.

"Yeah, bad idea. Why do holidays have to be so—"

"I don't know."

"So, it's okay if I drop you off?" I asked.

"Yeah. I'll just take the bus home tomorrow."

"That's good 'cause I don't want to stay out that long."

"Come on. You're gonna party tonight like it's 2003."

"Sure."

I drove up 30th Street—past the mall, past the old folks' home, past the liquor store. His friend lived in the apartment complex that my grandmother used to live in before she moved into assisted living on the other side of town. I pulled over to the side of the road to let my brother out.

"Bye Den," I said, cheerily.

"Bye. Happy New Year." He ran off like a six-year-old boy on the way to a ball game.

I headed over to Walnut Street where my friend lived. Instead of immediately going up to her house, though, I sat on the porch to enjoy the last cigarette of my life. I had planned it so that it was my lucky cigarette (the last of the pack), meaning I could make a wish. I wished that all these feelings of hopelessness and fear and uncertainty would go away. But I didn't finish smoking the cigarette. I could feel the tar and tobacco and everything else they pack into those things swirl around in my system and make my stomach feel sick and my heart beat faster. So I put it out and went upstairs. Would my wish come true anyway?

I was the first to get to Courtney's. A few of our friends had cancelled and a bunch were out of town. Eventually, a small, sad group of us, maybe six people, went to a bar on the Pearl Street Mall. It was okay, but I was still intent on leaving before midnight and also before people started getting too drunk or too high.

I looked at the clock on the wall and realized that it was 11:30—only a half an hour until midnight. I made some excuse to the group, and a few people acted jovially distressed—you know, the way people act when they're having fun and you aren't joining in. Courtney seemed genuinely sad to see me go, but I guess she could see I was fixed on leaving, so we all said bye and I left.

What I felt in the car ride home was relief. Relief that I still had it in me to be social. Relief that no one seemed to notice what was going on inside my head. And, yes, relief that I was going home.

I made it home and to the kitchen for water and to my bedroom and in my pajamas by five till. I walked over to the ledge where my book was sitting and picked it up. Just as I was about to settle into bed, I heard my phone ring.

It was Courtney, calling to wish me a Happy New Year. And it did make me happy that even though I went home early, opting out of a real celebration, I was still sort of a part of the night.

•

Father sat upright in his chair at their table in the crowded, lively restaurant.

"Honey," the woman—in her low voice—said to him, while leaning across the table, "tell me again where you grew up."

"Well, I grew up on a farm in Zimbabwe, but we moved to New York State when I was fourteen. But," he coughed, "my wife and I met in Europe, and we lived there for a few years."

"It's all so exotic," she replied.

"We also lived in Egypt for a couple years when Den and Bess were young."

"And you really want to go back, don't you? I mean, to Europe?"

"I've always wanted to live in France."

"I know I said this the other night, but I would love to live in Europe. I think it would be wonderful."

"We could really go, you know," he said intently.

"Do you really think so?"

"Yeah, why not? I've done it before."

"You must be so miserable here in Colorado."

"Not miserable...I've just always imagined my life different than this—"

"I know."

"We could buy a plot of land and start a farm. We could sell the produce locally. Or maybe we could buy a small vineyard," he said, with enthusiasm.

"Yeah, we could fix up the house, like in those books you read. I could learn French."

"If we did buy a vineyard, you could do the marketing for it."

"Denys, I'm behind you 100 percent. Whatever you want to do, I'll do it, too."

The server approached and asked if they wanted another bottle of wine. The woman shrugged her shoulders somewhat coyly, looking at Father. He nodded at the server.

The woman pushed her dinner—blackened catfish— around her plate and smiled at Father, who was about ten years older than she was, but still handsome and fairly young looking.

"Do you think your family knows?" she asked, though only nonchalantly. She didn't really want anything they had. That is, she didn't want to marry him. She just wanted to go out to dinner. And she was just a smile and a nod to him.

"No," he quickly responded. "No, not at all."

•

Den and I sat in the living room one night in January, books in hand. I was still reading *Heart of the Matter*; Den had opted for Jane Austen.

"It's ten-thirty. Where's Dad?" I asked, seemingly out of nowhere, with something like disbelief rising in my throat.

"I don't know. This is the third night this week." Den's tone matched mine.

A minute passed.

"Is he having an affair?" I offered.

"I guess," was his quick reply.

What my brother and I obviously both knew subconsciously for awhile finally came out in the open. My mom found out a few days after we did—though we hadn't told her. I guess my dad wasn't really hiding it anymore. The ensuing conflict made an already tumultuous household unbearable to live in, but I didn't have any money to move out. I had already decided to finish my master's program after all—but to take an extra semester and complete the program at a more manageable pace for me. But I still wasn't able to work full time, and, anyway, if I was feeling any better at all these days it was just because the shock of experiencing such intense feelings of anxiety and depression had begun to wear off.

I had been ready for a new life filled with wonderful possibilities. Suddenly, though, I'd started to wonder if that was what fate really had in store for me. From my parents' basement, it was hard to imagine myself in New York working at a publishing company or as a writer. Besides, so many people end up living miserable lives. Sometimes it seemed like so many people in my own extended family did. Why should I be any different? And I can say now that seeing my dad slowly pull away from us made it feel like I had no steady ground to stand on to fight all these fears that came popping up, one after another.

But I wanted so badly to get out of there. I just didn't think I could.

And then one day, a few weeks into the semester, I went to the financial aid office and took out a loan. I was moving out, again. And this time I wasn't ever going back.

•

Maybe a family system is like a living organism. Imagine an animal, a wolf, that's not very strong from birth. A back-of-the-pack type. Now imagine that the creature breaks its leg or something. Even though it's weak, it can probably nurse the break and keep up with the rest of the clan. But what if it gets bitten on that side too, just above the rib cage, before its leg heals? That might just be too much.

At the time, it never crossed my mind that my dad might have also been comparing his dreams to his reality. And if he was going through a hard time too, maybe he just didn't have the strength to take care of me. More than that, maybe seeing me, and my brother really, experiencing so many setbacks was just a little too much for him.

I had been so confused, hurt, and angry about everything that I couldn't even speak to my dad, let alone ask him for help of any kind. That feeling lasted for years. But in a weird way, it was a mixed blessing because it shocked me into taking complete responsibility for my own life, financially and otherwise. Maybe a father's breach of morality and loyalty wouldn't have affected someone else the way it affected me, but my dad had always quietly but surely taken care of us, all of us: my mother, my brother, and me. Well, almost all of us. The absence of my sister, I can say now, was a lesion that pointed to something deep and festering inside our home that would sooner or later erupt. As I look back, his affair probably propelled me around the long bend between adolescence and adulthood. My brother and sister also somehow flourished during this period, each of us realizing our own strengths and position within the family. And unlike so many marriages, my parents' didn't end in divorce. It wasn't a smooth process, but, maybe with the house to themselves and us kids standing on our own two feet, they could focus on themselves and their relationship again. It wasn't a smooth process, to say the least, but they worked it out in their own way.

One night in March, Courtney came over to my new apartment with a housewarming present. I didn't have a dining room table, or even a couch for that matter, so we sat on the floor eating an Amy's frozen pizza. By now she knew all about my dad and everything. I took a risk in telling her because she was a new friend, but it was worth it; now I had someone to talk to. It sounds cliché, but that was one of the best frozen pizzas I've ever had.

I know I should have moved out a long time before I did. But sometimes I guess we all run at the back of the pack, licking our wounds, fearing what's ahead and what's behind. Even though my family and I still weren't at our best, as least I could sit on the bare floor of my own apartment and feel, yes, unsure but also totally autonomous because—unlike that scared, grown-up kid living in the basement—I was free.

part:

4

LET THERE

BE

COHABITATION

Damn, are relationships ever frustrating. How do two people ever even decide they want to commit to each other forever—*forever*? To a lot of twentysomethings, it seems a million miles away. People suffer from much worse things than relationships—some starve while other folks buy designer doggie clothes, still others face war zones and crushing poverty—even still, it is the connection between two human beings that can cause the most angst and despair. And yet we get on the coaster again, because when relationships are good, they are very, very good...but when they are bad, they are horrid.

There's the lying and the cheating and the jealousy and the leaving. And how do two people know it is really love? Is there even such a thing as true love? Or, what do we do when we discover that the opposite sex doesn't really do it for us and never really has? How do we tell our friends and family that we're gay? And to circle back to Othello's desperate plight, Girl 1 has to worry about Girl

2 stealing Boy 1—but she also has to worry about Boy 2 pulling the same darn trick (wink, wink).

The options available to couples today make relationships vastly different than they were in the past. In the 1950s, close to half of all women were married by twenty, many of them already "with child" on their wedding days. Nowadays, more couples are choosing to live together before marriage, and a growing percentage are raising children outside of wedlock. Some women are having and raising children without cohabitating at all.

Two fools in lust no longer have to rush off to the altar. (Insert sigh of relief.) This opens up a lot of time for the searching of souls, the gazing at navels, the sowing of wild oats. Ironically, and sadly, some studies find that us young people who do rush into marriage and child bearing without qualms or complaints are significantly more likely to be in physically abusive relationships.

Still, what does a couple do if they accidentally find themselves pregnant? What if a woman is proposed to before she is quite ready, or living with a man who doesn't want to marry her? Kick the jerk out. Have the child. Get married. Stay. Move. Abort. Now that women enjoy more financial freedom and control over their own destinies, the choices can sometimes boggle the brain.

Of course, folks from the older generations often don't understand all the strum and drang. They married at twenty-one without once debating the pros and cons of a lifetime of commitment, and they did just fine, thank you very much (never mind that nearly 50 percent divorce rate). And they may be right, but that doesn't help when we're stuck in our own head, transfixed by different voices all barking contrasting orders regarding the strange and wondrous thing called love.

SALVATION
IN WORDPLAY

by *Justin Maki*

In the four years that I've known Shinji Keimura, a cheerful entrepreneur from Osaka, Japan, I have yet to figure out exactly what "entrepreneur" means in his case. I suppose my understanding of the word is shallow to begin with. Though I can follow his talk of language schools, science-lab technology, and international investment, I don't know how he turned these disparate ideas into a beautiful house, a silver BMW, and a viable free-wheeling life.

The first time we met was a chance encounter at my university computer lab, where I was working on the day Shinji came in from a conference hoping to check his email. He was only thirty-two years old at the time, and unlike the young, money-driven conservatives I'd met during my own brief attempt at business school, Shinji radiated a natural friendliness. A year later I dug out his business card and emailed to say that I'd been accepted to a teaching program in Japan and would arrive in Osaka shortly to begin work in a public high school. It turned out that his apartment was only twenty minutes by monorail away from mine. He treated me to sushi and dessert with his colleagues on one of my first nights in Japan, and a few months later invited me to his lavish wedding and reception on the top floor of the Hilton, overlooking all of Osaka City.

I knew nobody at the party but Shinji, so I kept to the periphery and marveled at the afternoon cityscape. All the way to the hazy blue hills in the distance, not a single foot of earth had been spared: Nothing escaped the crush of white and grey buildings, the dizzying jumble of rooftops and giant ads. I gazed down from the slightly tinted glass, taking in the miscellany, and tried to catch headlines scrolling quickly across the neighboring hotel's 35th-floor video screen.

Whenever I turned back to the party, I knew Shinji was somewhere in the sociable murmur; occasionally I would spot him in his tuxedo, moving easily from group to group, stopping just long enough to make pleasantries or create a roar of laughter. I couldn't imagine myself blending in so easily. Aside from the obvious language barrier, many of the guests were business students—which meant, in my mind, we had nothing in common. Eventually, Shinji's brother Daisuke drew me into conversation with a witty doctoral candidate from Austria, and the three of us ended up semi-included in a large, unfamiliar group of people who didn't seem to understand English. I still have a posed photo with myself in the middle, as if I were something more than a stranger to all the sharp, well-groomed young ladies and gentlemen behind me with their camera-ready grins.

Shinji came up beside me at the buffet a while after the group had dissolved. For the third time, he offered me encouragement. "There are many young ladies at this party," he smiled. "I think, they are eager to have an American boyfriend."

I nodded doubtfully, not sure what I could do. I had never yet had a girlfriend—American, Japanese, or otherwise—and liked to ease my pangs by thinking of love as too big and fortuitous a gift to fall under my conscious control. When it came, it would be a sudden, ineffable bond with a woman who truly understood me, and also had a great body. Or else it wouldn't come, in which case I was meant to be alone. I could live with that, too. But I didn't imagine myself putting forth any effort to get things started (such effort was superficial or desperate, I thought) and assumed that Shinji's encouragement, friendly but misguided, could only make me the token "American" in some mutually self-serving affair not much better than the skin trade.

Ignoring Shinji's advice, I moved around in a state of vague unease. Dessert was served. As a bridge between open, unstructured time and later formalities, Shinji kicked off a mingling game called "Happy Relations Bingo."

Everyone was given a golf pencil, a blank card, and a leisurely interval to circulate and fill the grid with names. Now I had a ready excuse to talk to people. I supposed that was good news. The bad news, of course, was that it still required a rogue effort at conversation with strangers. I figured that if I headed back toward the buffet for a second dessert, I could skip the game unnoticed.

My strategy worked for quite a while, until a trio of women in their forties, using a safety-in-numbers approach to mask sheer terror, surrounded me and asked my name. They giggled as I shook their hands. I wrote my name once on each of their cards while they, giggling again, took my card and pretended to fill up the blanks exclusively with their own names. It was awkward. So awkward, in fact, that it was laughable, even reassuring; watching them struck me with gentle chagrin, like what I would feel much later, watching an Italian movie in which the passionate main character shouts into a megaphone: "All shy people are shitheads!"

There was no reason for me to be so reserved. The women had each written their names once, and with a free space in the middle, I only had five more spaces to go. I handed my card to someone in a nearby group, who passed it among other people who were jotting distractedly and talking, and by the time my card returned to me all the spaces had been filled with Japanese names. I looked at the writing, then looked up at the nearby group and started to think aloud in my halting Japanese.

"So...for playing this game someone will...call out family names?"

"Yes," someone said.

"And I have family names on this card..."

"That's right," they said.

"But...I cannot read them."

The group erupted in laughter. Among its members were several young ladies in dark dresses and light shawls, one of whom caught my eye as she stepped forward to help. Smiling broadly, she took a minute translating the Chinese characters of family names into the easily pronounced Japanese syllabary. As I confirmed the readings, she and her friends welcomed me with a good vibe for conversation, so I ended up introducing myself and talking about my teaching position in a suburb of Osaka.

I noticed while answering the group's questions that the woman who'd first stepped forward to help stayed near me, seeming to take interest in what I said. She had dark eyes, a button nose, and bangs. Her pretty smile lingered. Soon she was the one asking most of the questions, and my answers were directed only to her. I was happy to make conversation; she was cute, easy to talk to, and apparently boyfriend-free. Her name was

Natsuko. Having graduated from college a few years earlier, she now worked full time in a bank. Not just any bank—the branch of UFJ that I passed every morning on my way to school, not more than a ten-minute walk from my apartment.

The two coincidences, from the improbable chance meeting with Shinji to this run-in with Natsuko, taken as two parts of the same bizarre sequence, were staggering. I felt a rush of confidence, assured that fate was on my side. It wasn't long before polite conversation picked up a flirtatious angle, a new overtone punctuated by signs of attraction, many of which I didn't catch until looking back on the night in retrospect. Nonetheless, I was doing all right. Neither of us had a winning combination of names on our cards, but we'd hit the main intended jackpot of Happy Relations Bingo; after the reception, Natsuko invited me to join her and a friend for coffee.

We found a table in a crowded Starbucks and took apart the gift packages given to all wedding guests on the way out. Among other small trinkets, there was a green silk handkerchief (used for tea ceremony, Natsuko told me) and colorful flower-shaped candies—"They are soaps!" Natsuko laughed. Upon more careful inspection, we guessed that they were, in fact, hard candies. I urged her to try eating one, and on behalf of all the children who'd ever had their mouths washed out with soap, I wanted to assure her facetiously that either way, soap or candy, *something* would come of it. I explained, or tried to, but like the Japanese of wedding-speech jokes that she'd tried to help me understand during the reception, explanation led to further confusion, which inspired our own random musings or unrelated wordplay. There was nothing wrong with that, but at moments I wondered if the spell would wear off once we ran out of basic get-to-know-you stuff to occasion it.

In the meantime, we managed to cruise past the lulls in conversation by encouraging Natsuko's quiet friend to give her opinions. Later Natsuko tried to speak English, but the outcome was usually the same as with my Japanese: an impasse of meaning, choppy changing of subjects, embarrassed laughter—almost in disbelief that we were together, two hours after meeting, still sitting over empty cappuccino cups and talking about nothing.

Natsuko's friend must have been bored by the time we left. We said goodbye in the train station, and when Natsuko encouraged me to stop by the bank where she worked, I promised that I would. Already I could see the day, how I would get out of school for a long lunch and go find her.

But I had my concerns, as well. The more I thought about it, the more nervous I became, unable to come up with a clear, detailed picture of what I should do inside the bank. My ability to be easygoing or charming was the most fickle variable in a wildly unpredictable destiny; the most I could do was clean up my apartment for luck, dress nicely, and walk out the door hoping something good would happen.

As soon as I stepped into the bank, I spotted Natsuko behind the counter. A second appraisal of her looks did not leave me disappointed. She glanced up a moment later, an unmistakeable flutter of excitement coming over her when she saw me. I was excited, too. I took a number and waited. But while sitting on the couch, I fell prey to sudden concern that my number would pop up over the wrong window. The nerve-racking lottery had so many potential outcomes, most of them wrong...so how would I handle it? Shake my head and request Natsuko? Tell someone else to go ahead? What if my messing with the flow of business embarrassed her or got her in trouble?

By the time I was beckoned to Natsuko's counter, my mind was still half-tangled in invisible scenarios. The relief I felt was not enough to bring me down from the tension; I opened a savings account without lapsing from a state of professional courtesy. When she cracked a small, flirtatious joke, I let it pass with a dull response. Even worse, I failed to ask for her number. I waited. I went back to the bank a week later, thinking I'd played it cool. I went back a third time, running out of plausible reasons, noticing that the excitement that had registered on her face the first time I'd come was no longer there. As I'd done with all my promising chances in college, I was losing it by moving too slowly. No, I had already lost it, and already half-knew it when I finally asked for her phone number.

"Oh, I am not hearing, on the phone," she answered sweetly. "I am always saying, 'What? Excuse me?'"

In the weeks that followed, as I looked back on the first night Natsuko and I had met, it was easy to understand why she liked me. When she first laid eyes on me at the reception, she'd seen a twenty-seven-year-old man. I had picked the color and cut of my suit with the same informed eye with which I'd chosen, among limitless options, Japan, and arranged my own employment, transportation, and living quarters. I was happy in my apartment, cooked for myself, kept things tidy. And on a certain day, there I was at a wedding party, flashing a grin. But she had no idea how I felt after we said goodbye; she didn't know that my apartment had a layer of clothes on the floor, plastic bags from the supermarket, empty orange juice cartons and sandwich wrappers and scattered plastic containers from ready-made sushi and box lunches; she didn't know that by the time I got back to this messy apartment, wearing a suit my mother had paid for, I was a twenty-two-year-old kid who had stumbled into a teaching program that gave me a free plane ticket to Japan, a fair job, and a convenient, furnished apartment. She had no idea that my application had been prompted by a whim, or that my decision two years earlier to take a Japanese language course had been an even bigger whim, prompted by nothing but a *Saturday Night Live* parody of a Japanese game show.

Even as I completed my degree and left campus for the world outside, I hadn't become any better at getting dates with attractive, intelligent women. I'd always hoped it would happen automatically, without much effort on my part, and had on those grounds kept waiting to see what would happen. The answer: nothing was happening. Except, of course, a sharpening awareness of my limitations as a twenty-two-year-old kid who'd never figured this stuff out.

I continued to see Shinji from time to time. Shinji's wife, an old friend of Natsuko, had the delicacy not to mention her to me, and Shinji himself was too busy. In addition to his other projects, he was now helping his brother Daisuke to open a Korean restaurant. Shinji had found a location in Takatsuki City, just north of Osaka, and planned a trip to Seoul and Cheju Island, Korea, for sensory inspiration.

Having, as always, multiple objectives in mind, Shinji also invited a younger colleague named Ken (affectionately called Ken-chan), who had no relation to the restaurant business. Ken was quite nearly as aimless as I was. He'd lived in America for a couple years before drifting back to Japan, but now seemed to be looking in earnest for a career. I didn't know how Shinji's business with Ken related to Korea.

And as a fourth member of the trip, for what purpose I couldn't imagine, Shinji invited me.

If my arrival in Osaka had seemed warmer because the language was familiar, my arrival in Seoul felt cold and foreign. All the bewilderment I'd spared myself by studying Japanese now hit me full-force in my total ignorance of Korean. Immersed in Hangul and heavy crowds, I struggled just to stay with our group—Shinji, Daisuke, Ken-chan, and I, led by a university student named Jin. Even after months of living in Seoul, Jin managed to get us lost almost right away and asked for directions hastily. If even he had trouble, I would have been clueless. And in a way, I was clueless: Since nobody in our group besides Shinji spoke English, I was at the bottom of the translation ladder. Our unofficial guide would translate from Korean to Japanese, and sometimes I would be left waiting for help in English. So I rarely had more than a vague notion of what we were doing or why.

Jin, a third-generation Korean-Japanese who had grown up in Kyoto, negotiated a deal for our hotel rooms, then took us to a hole-in-the-wall restaurant across town, a local place that was noisy and bustling, a relief from the night chill. We were seated in a cramped corner and ate octopus stew with garlic and greens, so spicy that we gulped cold saké to cool our mouths, then had a second course of octopus legs still writhing around on the plate. Ordering was completely beyond me; the menu was all in Korean, and, as at the hotel, our guide would translate Korean into Japanese, and I would still be partially at a loss. Other times I would miss the drift of conversation, and find myself going long periods of time without paying attention. After we finished eating, I tried to concentrate on listening again. I heard Shinji say to our guide in

Japanese: "All right, then. Let's go to that place you were telling us about."

We needed two taxis because there were five of us. Our guide hailed the first cab, spoke to the driver, and then hailed another cab for himself and Ken-chan. As we rode along, I thought about the driver knowing exactly where we were going, Shinji and Daisuke having some idea from earlier conversation, while I had no clue. I just watched the dark highway unfolding in front of us, with block after block of enormous, dimly lit apartment buildings. There were red neon crosses mounted here and there, at various heights, and the moon looked almost orange from air pollution.

It was a long ride, but finally we got out near some fruit stands beside a big shopping center. When our guide caught up with us, he mentioned neither the fruit market nor the shopping center; we followed him through a few back streets where the buildings were more run-down, where there was more debris and dust. Then we came to a narrow street where scantily clad women were hanging out in glass booths. Even though it was cold, most of them had the sliding door open and stood there smoking or talking to men. Each booth had spotless glass panels and a few things to make it look like a barber shop—a chair or two, a radio, mirrors, beauty supplies. Not that there was much effort put into deception. These women were clearly waiting for men, and as Jin explained, the symbol of two barber poles right next to each other, rotating inward, tells you that this is not the neighborhood for a haircut.

My first response was a sort of confused excitement, fueled by opportunism and less-than-detached curiosity. I eyed some of the sexier girls, smooth-skinned, bored, in the peach glow of their booths. Most of them were in their late teens or early twenties, rail-thin, wearing skimpy tops and tight polyester pants, or loose silk that hung all the way to the soles of their big blockish shoes. I gave one or two of the women a second look, but I still didn't want to be a guy who resorted to the sex industry. Quickly I found myself a bit embarrassed to be there, and had an urge not to linger. But it was not a completely simple decision—I wasn't alone.

Daisuke approached the first woman we saw and grabbed her breasts; she recoiled angrily. He gave an orange to the next one, and patted her ass, which she didn't seem to mind. As we wandered along this street and a couple more like it, some of the women called out insistently to the Japanese guys, and tried to speak Japanese. Very few attempted English. Shinji asked one woman how much she would charge me, but I immediately turned her down—wondering if it had been, more than principle, the fact that I didn't find her attractive. Another woman punched the glass when Daisuke leered at her. Our guide asked her why she was upset, and translated what I thought was an obvious reason. Finally, Daisuke bought thirty minutes for $55 and went into a booth, behind the curtain into the bedroom. Ken-chan took a similar deal. Sometimes one of the red neon crosses would appear above everything as we walked. The orange-tinted moon was nearly full. Shinji and I went to a nearby coffee shop to wait.

"Why don't you go take a lady?" he asked me. I could have asked him the same thing, but for the memory of a beautiful wedding ceremony I'd attended the year before.

"It's too risky," I answered.

"Ah, I know. Maybe, you get some disease."

That was one concern, of course, but other factors were just as important. An inkling of religious condemnation of any sex outside of marriage made me pause, as did a revulsion at sex as business, and a fear of making myself a target for crime. But already I was arguing with myself. Wasn't it possible that my concerns, for all their appeals to logic, amounted to no more than trifles on the verge of a much-needed rite of passage? If I had a nudge, something to make me feel stupid for my hesitation, maybe I would go through with it. And wouldn't I be better off? As I'd learned the hard way with Natsuko, even if fate leads you to water, it's *you* who has to drink.

After twenty minutes, our guide went out and came back with Ken-chan, who greeted us with a goofy look on his face and ordered a cup of coffee. Daisuke should have been finished as well, but our guide wasn't certain where he had gone in, and Shinji seemed a bit hazy on it, too.

"I remember the place," I said.

Shinji and I set out, and I walked right to it. A woman there told us in Japanese that Daisuke would be done in ten minutes. There were booths on both sides, and the street was so narrow that we had to step up on a tiny curb to let taxis pass. We stood there for a while, looking around, waiting.

A woman behind us suddenly jerked her door open and yelled at us in Korean for blocking the way. She appeared to be a manager, mid thirties, and for some reason she had a small dog inside her sweater. I only realized it was a dog when the bulge started yapping, and a tiny head popped up under the woman's chin. As we started to move, another small dog jumped out through the sliding door and bit my shoe, undoing the laces, which was even more comical than the woman's barking belly. We relocated to a dim section a few yards down, stifling laughter.

While I tied my shoelace, the whole situation seemed ridiculous to me. Either you could fulfill your desire and regret it later, or not fulfill your desire and regret *that* later, or go either way and try not to regret the outcome. Who says hindsight will be accurate anyway? It can only be the way that it was. I hadn't so much as touched a woman except for the occasional hug or handshake. Maybe I would never have a chance. Obviously the girls who were pretty now would get less pretty, while the ones who stayed pretty would be more and more in demand, and likely to have a better time with men who were experienced. I faced losing odds. And as for having sex, doing it with a woman who wasn't pretty was simply out of the question.

So here they were, right before my eyes, pretty ladies, smooth skin, willing bodies.... What was stopping me?

When he came out of the booth a few minutes later, Daisuke was grinning at us. He apologized for keeping me waiting.

"Oh," I said blankly. "It's all right."

After returning to the others, we sat for a while over cups of coffee. There was a discussion that I didn't understand, other than a few details: Shinji's brother had rushed to kiss her and take her clothes off, but kissing is not allowed and the women take their own clothes off. She got irritated. There was nothing in the room but a bed, a little bigger than a single. Nowadays there are many loan words in daily use in Japan, words like "hamburger" and "video" that have been approximated with Japanese sounds (han-baa-gaa and bideo). I learned that "fellatio" goes by the same rule. And many Japanese people seem to know the word "fuck."

We took a cab to the city center and walked back to our hotel. As we went past bus stops and shopping centers, all the girls in advertisements looked the same to me as the whores.

＊

Our plan for the next day was to visit the campus of Yosei University and see our unofficial guide's dorm room. I got up late and met Shinji and the others at our small hotel's breakfast table as they finished their coffee and toast. I was feeling much better than the night before; there was even a cute girl sitting a few chairs away from us, and I started up a conversation with her in Japanese. She was from Aomori Prefecture, traveling alone. I had heard that Aomori, the northernmost prefecture in Honshu, was beautiful during the winter, a great place to bathe in hot springs and drink saké as the snow fell. Before we could talk for more than a minute, though, my traveling companions were getting up to pay the bill. I had to finish my coffee and leave.

The morning was grey and chilly, like the day before. Patches of snow and ice on the ground. Traffic was heavy at 9 a.m., on a road lined with drab buildings and leafless trees. I hadn't seen many destitute or homeless people, but when we stopped at a convenience store, a miserable-looking man in sweats followed us in to ask for money. The manager grabbed him, but he stood there obstinately, with a grimace on his face, glaring at me. I looked at him squarely, not knowing what else to do. Finally, the manager made him leave and apologized to us. We left and walked a few more blocks, past a shopping arcade with big "2002" plaques in the sidewalk. From the city center we caught a cab.

Our friend's dorm room was so small that five of us could barely fit inside; two sat on the single bed, one sat at his desk, I stood behind the desk, and the student himself had to stand in the doorway. A Korean prostitute might have fit in the middle, but she would have to leave her big shoes in the hall. We took off before long, and after a tour of the hilly campus, we spent the afternoon wandering through outdoor markets full of clothes, art, and souvenirs. We ate ramen for lunch and had grilled octopus slices and thin cakes of dried fish as we walked, washing it down with saké from paper cups; then we stopped at a coffee shop for tea and snacks. After our walk, we ended up at a big restaurant.

"What? You're hungry again?" I asked Shinji as we were ushered into a private room with cushions around a low table.

"Aren't you?" he replied.

The meal included several courses of noodles and stews and spicy kim-chi. I don't remember it clearly because I couldn't eat very much. I kept falling out of the conversation, unable to catch the Japanese. Accepting the saké and beer that came my way, I became absorbed in my own thoughts. I was thinking about prostitutes.

It's possible to make up a logical framework for any bad decision; I was tiptoeing along the border. Should there be prostitutes in the world? Sexuality can't be suppressed, so why not have experts? And why not go to an expert if so inclined?

I was also thinking about a temple we'd visited briefly. The outside was under construction, but the inside was a huge red hall with a seated monk facing the altar, singing some kind of chant. Dozens of people were kneeling on mats, worshipping silently. I wondered what they believed? Did they consider life to be an illusion? Would they tell you that there are many lives in one life, as well as many sets of lives for one soul? I was beginning to think that way, independent of religion. The art of being alive, it seems, is demonstrating that you don't take things too seriously, showing that you want to be here, want to be taking risks, experimenting, winning, and losing. The best people roll with the punches, and know how to play.

The meal was over, and everyone was leaning back, satisfied. Shinji was speaking dreamily about something I didn't understand. He turned to me and spoke English:

"Do you know what I mean, if I say a 'win-win situation?' Maybe the five of us have a unique network, so we can get together in the future and have a good time, and do business."

Yeah. I thought about it a moment. Such a thing seemed likely, but it seemed more likely that I would fall out of the loop by then. I was no good for business, too restless for responsibility. Though I'd grown up poor, my mother always kept the financial burden off me personally, to the extent that I could follow my temperament, opt out of structured work, quit business school—and end up not a drifter begging change from tourists, but a college graduate with a comfortable job overseas.

From my standpoint it was all coincidence, unaccountable good fortune. The job and work visa were mine for three years. But then what? If I couldn't shake the inertia of a confused kid, how could I ever learn to fend for myself? Or maybe another coincidence would arise to keep me going. Maybe Shinji would give me a menial job, and I would be flying back to Japan to work this menial job, because I'm an idiot like most people and I need to work for somebody.

"2002," the sidewalk read in big numbers. The year the World Cup came to Seoul. The year I left America for the first time, with a free ticket to Osaka and no idea what would happen. 2002. The year in my memory getting dirty, trod upon, obsolete—numbers in the sidewalk. I could feel the irony of that flight back to Japan, the same route but without excitement or wonder, just a ceaseless mulling over whatever had gone wrong.

I was dwelling on sullen images, missing even more of the conversation. Shinji was still elaborating dreamily when I tried to listen in. He spoke as if selling a vision. The others nodded like there was nothing they wanted more, while I barely had any idea what he was talking about.

Outside, we parted with our unofficial guide. Before saying goodbye, Ken-chan took out a pad to write something that Jin pronounced carefully for him. Daisuke joined in, rehearsing the words with Ken-chan several times. As we walked through the city center in the general direction of our hotel, the two of them hurried forward in search of a taxi.

Shinji had not mentioned any other plans for the evening. I hoped that he would wander around with me for a while, failing anything else.

"I'm a bit tired. Not tired. What is the word, you taught me before?"

"Lazy."

"That's it. I feel lazy," he said. I realized with horror that he was thinking of going to bed already.

"You don't want to walk around? You don't want to shoot pool? You don't want to fuck a Korean whore? You don't want to do anything?" I kidded him.

"Do you want to go back to the ladies?" Shinji asked me.

I was a bit drunk and impatient at his misunderstanding. It was our last night in Seoul; all I wanted was not to forfeit it. "If they're going back to that area, that's fine with me. Maybe I'll wander around and meet them somewhere," I said.

"Maybe, if you go to that place, you will enter the booth."

It could happen, I thought. It was just what I needed. A way, at last, to stir myself to action, to force the culmination I wanted so badly.... But I was getting ahead of myself. We were still behind Daisuke and Ken-chan, on the same road that led to our hotel. I was a bit unclear on what was happening.

"Are they whoreward bound?" I asked. After re-phrasing my question, I found out that yes, the two of them were definitely headed in that direction. And I was welcome to join them. Presently, they spotted an empty cab.

I thought about the number of lives in a life. I thought about the need for experimentation and sheer guts. I thought about my dear neighbor, and our first long discussion in over a week, the night before my departure for Seoul. "Four days isn't very long," I'd told her.

"Four days can be a lifetime," she'd said.

As Daisuke and Ken waited for me, I remembered all the regrets that came from inaction, all the missed opportunities. And yet, I had a feeling that impatience and overreaction were just as bad. Simply put, both choices were wrong. The considerations were a muddle. Who in the world had time, or the self-control, to sort them out without experience?

In the end, I suppose I knew that veering from one extreme to the other wouldn't change anything. And in retrospect, I can see that what I needed were more experiences getting to know interesting women like Natsuko and the girl from Aomori, not experiences taking advantage of prostitutes. But all this happened in a few seconds: I looked at Daisuke and Ken, and gave my answer. I watched the door close. The taxi disappeared.

I could have wandered off alone at that point, but Shinji warmed to the idea of shooting pool, so we stopped by a busy pool hall that had only one table with pockets. For a while I picked up a sort of brusque good humor. I was driving the balls home and acting like Tom Cruise in "The Color of Money." I explained at length, stopping just short of Simon & Garfunkel, what I had meant by "whoreward bound," and why it was extraordinarily clever.

MARY'S BED

by Rebecca Landwehr

Mary and I were in bed when she asked. Colorado's summer sun had already forced itself through her home-made curtains, and the paper had arrived with a thud. We were chatting about our brunch options, and it seemed the day had all the markings of an indulgent Sunday of lounging. Instead, Mary asked *the* question, the one that had been rattling around in my head for weeks. Our day was shot.

"What if nobody ever loves you like that again?" I froze—she can't be serious. But the look of concern on her face confirmed this was indeed an earnest question coming from my closest friend. In that moment, by actually saying the words, she'd given life to my biggest fear. Like a fairy godmother whose well-intentioned gift will inevitably backfire, Mary apparently sealed my fate.

It was July 1999. I was twenty-eight years old and had decided to leave Dave, my high school sweetheart, after a ten-year relationship. Even though she clearly thought I'd just ditched the only man who would ever love me, Mary supported me unconditionally during the breakup.

Being modern twentysomethings, Dave and I had lived together. We shared an apartment, a car, an incredibly nasty cat, and about $15,000 in credit-card debt. Even among our freewheeling set of spendy friends, the debt was impressive. Together we'd racked up the plastic with a passion for sushi and Kate Spade purses (mine) and two solid years of Playstation-playing unemployment (his). Dave had wrecked his credit rating in college and didn't have a job, therefore leaving him credit impaired. So I carried all the debt in my name. My justification was the hope that he was secretly saving his pennies to buy me a diamond ring. It was going to be any day, I was sure of it.

So for the four years from my twenty-fourth birthday until our ten-year anniversary, which we celebrated about a month before we broke up, I was in a constant state of romantic readiness. My proposal could be around any corner, and I was always ready to squeal a, "Yes, of course I will marry you!" should the opportunity arise. I was like a diamond sleuth; every restaurant meal could be a "pop-the-question" occasion. Perhaps a weeknight stop for sushi with a ring served alongside my himachi sashimi? Fabulous. I could carry that theme into our wedding reception and have a sushi chef during the cocktail hour. I was big on the food proposals, and every Valentine's Day I would gingerly pick at my tiramisu, certain there was a diamond hiding in there somewhere.

Holidays were the worst. I imagined my Christmas gift delivered on bended knee in his parents' New Jersey home. That one was my favorite proposal scenario. Then we could immediately share the news with our family and hometown friends. (Plus it would be convenient for wedding dress shopping back at Kleinfeld's, the famous

Brooklyn bridal shop.) The anticipation wrecked my social calendar. I couldn't even go to a baseball game without wistfully looking at that scoreboard hoping the lights would spell out a, "Will you marry me, Rebecca?" I figured it would come in the third or fourth inning. Despite my constant state of proposal awareness, I was sure I could feign gleeful surprise and a good dose of tears for the benefit of the fans who would surely buy us rounds of 16-ounce Budweisers in celebration. But in hindsight, baseball games weren't all that romantic for Dave and I. Mostly we'd get drunk and by the eighth inning we'd be taking pot shots at each other. Make that me taking the pot shots at him: I was pissed off and he didn't know why. More than a few times we left the field yelling at each other, and there was that particularly unfortunate incident on a bus ride home that none of our friends (not to mention the driver) will likely forget.

As time wore on, my imagined proposals started getting less and less grand. Same goes for my dream engagement ring. At first I pictured a flawless, emerald-cut diamond in a tasteful one-karat weight. My fingers are long, you see, so they could carry off the stone's harsh shape. In time my tastes were downgraded to a cheaper, but still stylishly square, princess cut. I passed along industry know-how to Dave: "Did you know you can get a bargain with the stones that are just under a karat because size-conscious guys will always buy up?" By the end, had my boyfriend simply paused his session of "Madden 99" on the Playstation and handed me a hunk of jade on a piece of wire I would've been happy. I would've said yes. I would've been engaged.

Everyone has their one danger zone. For a lot of people it's between twenty-seven and twenty-nine years old, that time when you start to get a lot of big envelopes crammed into your tiny apartment mailbox. Your peers are getting married and the pressure to couple-up mounts. That pressure hit me hard and for all the wrong reasons.

Of our friends, Dave and I had known each other since we were kids, we'd dated longer than anyone we knew, and I thought that meant I should be having a wedding. It was my turn. For those reasons my danger zone was earlier than many, from twenty-four to twenty-eight years old. I was so focused on getting married and starting the rest of my life that I completely ignored the rut where our relationship had landed. We started bringing out the worst in each other. His lack of initiative brought out my bossy nature. My bitchy accusations only increased his insecurities about his job, his social stature, and his hairline. But why did I push these truths aside? Simple. I wanted to have a baby before I was thirty. That meant a year of engagement, a year to be married, and a year to buy a house before I could get pregnant. The changing of the seasons were hard on me, for every spring that Dave didn't propose I knew that meant no summer wedding the following year—the best wedding venues would surely be booked a year out.

While I was tapping my foot waiting for a diamond ring, my personality became uglier by the day. When coworkers would show up on Monday morning with a certain glow and a shiny ring, I could pretend to be happy, swallowing my jealousy only to take it out on Dave when I got home. Of course I never said anything directly, instead I'd complain about his shoes being left in the living room or nag him to clean up his breakfast dishes, while pouring myself a glass of wine. For every dinner date when I came home without a diamond ring, I would find more qualities in Dave that drove me crazy. Our relationship was deteriorating, yet I was too consumed with getting married to face it. I'd invested this much time in Dave, and if we didn't get married how was I ever going to stay on my schedule?

But we obviously weren't having any fun together. And we certainly weren't having sex. I had enlisted the habit of going to bed early and pretending I was asleep to avoid all but the occasional obligatory romps. But we discussed none of this. Instead, we worked all day (mostly me), came home, ate dinner, had a beer or did the occasional bong hit, and turned on the TV. I'll never know how Dave felt during the last year of our relationship: Was he comfortably clueless? Or was he smarter than me? Could the real reason he never proposed be because deep down he knew it would be a terrible mistake?

It hadn't always been like this. Dave and I met in the fifth grade. We both played the trumpet at different elementary schools and our paths crossed at All-City Stage Band, where the best kids from each elementary school played in one premier band. He was the total grade-school package—cute, smart, and funny. Plus he was from a different school so he had an air of mystery. He arrived at band practice with an arsenal of wisecracks that always made me giggle. In junior high and high school we both continued our musical careers and sat next to each other for five years of band practices. Almost every day we commiserated about teachers, talked about parties, compared friends, and complained about our parents. But mostly what I remember was that Dave always made me laugh.

We were band geeks, but somehow we thought we were the coolest band geeks around. Dave and I only started dating during the last months of our senior year. We fell in love hard and fast that summer, although I'm pretty sure I'd been in love with him since the fifth grade. That final summer of high school before the scary uncertainty of college we latched onto each other, confounding our friends and family alike.

We started out at separate colleges but eventually I transferred to the University of Colorado to be with Dave.

We were the stable couple among our rowdy friends and, aside from one notorious Super Bowl Sunday argument, Dave and I were solid throughout our college years—we shared a lot of fun times. It was after graduation that the relationship started to crumble.

I pounded the pavement and took a low-paying job at a business newspaper. Every morning at 7:10 I rode the bus to Denver and worked my ass off in my entry-level job in journalism. I was broke, but I was thrilled to have a paycheck and a byline. Dave, on the other hand, floundered. He had no clue about a career path. His dream was to make movies, but he'd somehow talked himself out of that possibility years ago. I can't remember if he even had a resume or if he looked for jobs, what I do recall is that for two years Dave held court on our sofa and played video games all day. His mom sent checks to cover his rent, but most of our social life went on the plastic. During that time our relationship started to fizzle. His self-esteem was shot and my bitterness was born—I wasn't happy pulling long nights on the job while he watched *Ren & Stimpy* reruns. A few of my girlfriends noticed our problems and asked me about moving on. But at that point I didn't think I could break up with Dave in his state. He was unemployed and miserable—how could I do that to him?

Eventually Dave's brother got him a job in Denver. Things were starting to look up. He was earning steady money and regaining his self-confidence, not to mention his sense of humor. But looking back, at that point I was already finished with the relationship—it just took a few more years for me to realize it. I'm not sure why I didn't break up with Dave then. I guess I was scared. I'd always assumed Dave was the guy I was suppose to end up with. We'd been together almost every single day from fifth grade until our mid twenties. We had a shared history that I would never find in another man. No one else could laugh about the dorky trombone player in that fifth grade band, or the night we stole the keg from a rival high school party, or the first time we saw Phish at Red Rocks. And probably, like Mary said, I was afraid no one would ever love me like that again. How could they? No one could compete with the years that Dave and I had logged.

Once Dave and I hit year number seven in our relationship, I started making snide, offhand comments about never dating someone for more than ten years. It was my ultimatum, although even I wasn't sure I'd follow through. Besides, there was no way he'd make me wait that long. He did. And on that June day he handed me two-dozen roses and a card. In it he wrote sheepishly, "Happy anniversary, you're not going to break up with me are you?" We both knew.

The breakup started with a conversation. It took about two or three of those conversations before we accepted this was really happening. Then there was two weeks of walking around each other in the apartment, sleeping on the couch, and coming home late before it was clear that I had to leave. And that was when Mary took me in. A smart, single woman, she had purchased her tiny condo three years earlier. It was a one-bedroom so Mary shared her bed with me for that whole summer. We had been friends since high school; she was friends with Dave, too. So when Dave and I decided to move to Denver, we conveniently chose an apartment kitty-corner from her condo. Of course now that I was dismantling the relationship, the location was no longer prime real estate. It meant I often found morning notes on my windshield. Depending on Dave's mood the previous night, his notes varied. Some begged for a second chance, other days it was pure notebook-paper venom.

At first Mary and I played sitcom roles, where I was the conflicted one—broken hearted and guilty, yet thrilled to be free. She was the more experienced one, dispensing advice over white wine and triangles of Brie. Then there was that Sunday morning in bed. "What if nobody ever loves you again?"

Once my breakup was settled, Mary put her condo on the market. She was moving back east to be with her long-distance boyfriend. Of course she was too smart to move in with him; Mary would sell her condo and live with her parents while she and Tom gave their relationship a real try. She was listing the place for $65,000 but would've let me have it for $60,000. "You can afford this, you could even put your credit-card debt into the mortgage and still afford this." But I was short sighted and simply couldn't imagine buying property across the street from my ex. It would be too awkward. So instead, Mary started scouring the papers looking for a cheap, safe, yet fabulous place for my next move.

During that summer, Mary decided it was time I learn to become independent. A lot of my schooling centered on money. It was insane that I was spending $48 on hair conditioner; she said the Aveda Cherry Almond Bark had to go. I was now a Salon Selectives girl. She took me to T.J. Maxx and showed me how to shop the cheaper, juniors' section for the real bargains. She showed me how to enlist her patented strategy at the grocery store and organize my lunches for the workweek, saving precious pennies not to mention calories. I could still eat sushi, but only at happy hour when it was discounted.

One night, over buy-one-get-one-free drinks at our neighborhood bar, Mary gave me her theory on my summer. "You know, that's why this all happened for you," she said, sipping a martini. "You turned twenty-eight right before you left him. It's Saturn's Return." As

Mary explained it, Saturn's Return is the cosmic phenomenon when the stars literally align themselves in the same pattern as the year you were born. It supposedly happens every twenty-eight years and usually means a year of great change and cosmic energy—good and bad. For me, that summer of my twenty-eighth year, Saturn's Return, was when I learned how to live my own life. At first it was the little things: I took out my own trash and killed my own spiders. Soon the big picture came into focus. Now I was responsible for the state of my life. I could no longer blame Dave for a cluttered house or a big credit-card statement. I couldn't blame him for a stalled future. Everything was up to me—my dreams, my career, and my adult opportunities. I had been waiting for a wedding to signal the beginning of "the rest of my life." In reality, the rest of my life had already started, I just hadn't noticed. I was idling at the green light, blaming the traffic for the delay.

When my mother was twenty-eight, I was a one-year-old baby. She quit her job as a computer programmer for Westinghouse and was busy managing a home on my father's graduate-school stipend. She cared for a young child, clipped coupons, and tried to forge new friendships with other moms in the neighborhood. At night, after putting her baby to bed, and doing the evening's dishes, she typed my dad's thesis on a manual typewriter. At twenty-eight, she was creating the foundation of her family.

For me, the dismantling of what I so desperately thought would become my family actually wasn't so different. I was establishing my own foundation as a person, not half of a couple—but as myself. It took me twenty-eight years to become responsible for my own life. And ultimately, this individual I was becoming would be the foundation of my own future marriage and family. Maybe it wasn't Saturn's Return. Who knows what happened to me that year, but Mary's theory provided a tangible explanation for the fabulous chaos I found myself in.

It didn't take long till Mary found my new apartment. It was cheap, big, and funky, and I cried when the landlady handed me the lease. Even though I'd fallen out of love years earlier and I didn't regret the decision to leave Dave, seeing my name alone on the lease was my last step in moving on. This concerned the landlady who thought I'd ditch the lease and go back to my boyfriend, but Mary smoothed things over, handed me a pen from her purse, and forced me to sign the lease before the landlady changed her mind.

Before she left town, we made a list of all the things I would buy from her—silverware, dishes, TV, sofa, a chair, even her spice rack with all the spices included. I wrote a single check for the contents of her single-girl life. There was even this chic little "Do It Herself" toolbox with the basic supplies I needed for household maintenance. She was moving on with her life, and while we didn't know it at the time, she was months away from her own engagement. As for me, I was finally starting life on my own. The biggest single item on that list was her bed. That same place where Mary wondered aloud whether I'd just discarded my only chance at love. It's a really nice bed, a Sealy, and (of course) she'd gotten a great deal on it. It had a warranty and everything. It's been ten years since she bought it and it's still firm yet comfy. When I eventually got married and my husband and I merged our world into his small condo, I donated most of Mary's single-girl supplies to a twenty-four-year-old coworker, a guy also named Dave. But I convinced my husband that my bed was better than his lumpy king-size mattress. Mary's bed is the one we kept. It's here that my husband, our dog, and my six-year-old stepdaughter snuggle under the covers contemplating Saturday morning breakfast. Now the question in bed is far less ominous: "Who wants pancakes?"

THE RING

by Jennifer Banash

I hated my bridal bouquet. Not so much the flowers themselves, but what they came to represent. My mother had
this idea of saving my bouquet, mounting it behind glass
and securing the dried, withered flowers, their colors
faded, beneath a golden frame. As I listened to her voice
over the telephone, winding the cord around my arm rest-
lessly, I thought of butterflies pinned under glass, their
wings outstretched in a parody of flight. She had, she
told me, found a company that specialized in this kind of
preservation. Apparently (and for reasons I couldn't quite
fathom), it was very popular. "You'll have it forever!" she
exclaimed, her voice chipper, so full of happiness that I
couldn't bring myself to say no to her.

When it arrived four months later, I was already well
on my way to being divorced. The "preserved" bouquet
came packaged elaborately in a huge, brown cardboard
box that took up most of one wall in our living room.
When I removed it from the box, I gasped. It was like
unearthing a corpse, the limbs pale and lifeless after so

much time spent underground. I had already begun the seemingly insurmountable task of moving, and the room was still and quiet, almost empty. I could see my reflection in the glass hovering over the Casablanca lilies I had chosen so carefully, and I could almost smell their white, waxy aroma, the cloyingly sweet smell of rot and regret rising into the desert night.

I came from a wealthy New York family—generous with money, but tight with feelings, and completely physically abusive. I ran away from the violence, the shame—and home—when I was fifteen years old. I clawed a life for myself out of nothing and buried the rage I felt at my parents, at my misspent childhood, deep inside me. As a result, in my early twenties I was obsessed with building the family I never had, making some kind of safe haven for myself in a world where I felt perpetually unsafe and ill-equipped. I'd never been given the tools to deal with the rudimentary aspects of daily life. I didn't know how to balance a checkbook, I was a terrible driver, and I was woefully unskilled at interpersonal relationships—I didn't know how to be a "team player," as my bosses were constantly telling me, usually right before I got fired. I was just trying to make it through, one day after the next. I see now that I was just trying to survive.

I was twenty-four. I had managed to graduate from Arizona State with a degree in photography. I made collages and wrote poetry. I dreamed of writing a novel. Mostly I just *dreamed*. I had a good job working for ABC-TV in Phoenix, a steady live-in boyfriend, and a close network of friends to hold me up. Life was pretty good, until my boyfriend asked me to marry him. It should've been a dream come true for someone who was desperately looking for closeness. In spite of the fact that all I wanted was some kind of emotional security, alarm bells rang out in my brain with disquieting clarity when he slid the ring across the dinner table one night, my heart beating so fast that I couldn't breathe. That should've been the time to gently, but firmly, say no, take him by the hand and tell him that I wasn't ready to belong to anyone yet, that I wasn't sure if I even belonged to myself. But I didn't do any of those things. I put the ring on my finger and smiled, wiping away fake tears from my eyes, and accepted.

Looking back on it, I think that the crisis of my twenties lay in the fact that I thought I should want what I was supposed to want, what was normal: A husband, a house, kids, a career. In reality, I had no idea what I wanted, or needed for that matter. I was raised with no prospects for my future, raised to marry a rich man—just like my mother. This way just seemed easier, like swallowing a spoonful of honey sprinkled with broken glass.

And there was the ring. It was the ring of my dreams. I have never been the sort of girl who covets diamonds the size of robin's eggs. I am in love with history, tradition, jewelry that speaks quietly, that does not shriek its intentions. We were browsing in an antique store one lazy Sunday afternoon when I first saw it nestled in a glass case—echoes of Sleeping Beauty—encased in a bright blue velvet box. The ring shone like the light from a dead star, incandescent. It literally called to me, and I wanted nothing more than to slide it onto my finger and run out of the store. It was white gold with a delicately etched band, an art deco piece. The diamond in the center was raised up on a sharply edged platform of silvery-gold, the stone sparkling in the sunlight. It wasn't the biggest diamond I'd ever seen, or the brightest, but it had a quiet dignity that simply sang to me. I stopped in front of the case and gazed at it, holding my breath. I pointed out the ring when my boyfriend came up behind me, and we both admired it, his hand resting quietly on the small of my back. But at seven hundred dollars, I knew that it was more than he could ever afford.

When he pulled the box out of his pocket six months later, I knew immediately what was inside and how much it had cost him. He'd worked all summer at one terrible job after another to buy me that ring. It was as if he was sliding his whole heart to me across the table. When I put the ring on my finger, it felt as if it had always been there. I looked down at its sparkling white beauty and my face flushed—I immediately began to feel guilty. The fact was I had been cheating on my boyfriend for months, and I felt incapable of stopping or of telling him the truth. It wasn't that I didn't love him—far from it. He was gorgeous, smart, kind, and attentive—just the type of guy I thought I should someday marry. I admired him for his kindness, his talent. He wasn't rich, but he was gentle and loving, and I felt safe with him.

The problem was that I just wasn't sexually attracted to him. That spark that everyone talks about wasn't there. As far as I know, everything was just fine on his end of things, but during sex I was decidedly bored, staring at the ceiling and waiting for it to be over. Whatever the cause, I knew I was in trouble. *Big* trouble. I had found the perfect guy—a guy who would hold my hair out of my face when I threw up from food poisoning, a guy who made me dinner not just once a week but practically every night, a guy who cried when he watched *Gone With the Wind*— and I didn't want to marry him. I'm not sure I wanted to marry *anyone*. So instead of confronting him and ending things, I did what any sensible twentysomething girl in my position would've done: I ignored the situation. And I cheated—over and over again.

I liked cheating. I liked lying in the darkness of a guy's bedroom, the late afternoon Arizona sunlight blazing away outside the drawn curtains, the only sounds in the room being the wet, sucking sounds of sex and guttural moans of pleasure. I liked the intensity of it—how much these men wanted me, and the fact that I didn't have to make it work in the real world. There *was* no real world in those dark rooms, and the ring winking brightly on my finger cancelled out any chance of one barging into my fantasy life. I liked how well-used my flesh felt as I pulled my dress back on as the sun set high in the sky, how tired and sore my muscles were—as if I'd just returned from the gym. My body felt languid, full of warm liquid. I smiled as I drove home, looking at my face in the rearview mirror, rubbing my reddened lips, applying lip gloss, and checking my face for any signs of guilt. I felt none. I needed those afternoons. They were as imperative to my well being as air or water. They made my life—and what was happening to it—bearable.

By the time I arrived home, I was as calm as if I'd just taken a sedative. When I opened the door to the smell of dinner in the oven, music blaring from the stereo, the sounds of life, of *home*, something inside of me relaxed in relief. As I walked toward my fiancé, I opened my arms, encircling them around his bare-chested torso as he stirred a pot on the stove, whispering into his hair. I would disappear into the bathroom and shower, the water pounding down on my head and shoulders. I was almost okay with what I was doing. *Almost.*

There were a succession of men—maybe five total that year before the wedding. It was a kind of serial monogamy I was practicing—intense affairs, both emotionally and physically, that ran their course over a few months. I liked the fervor; I wanted more and more. It was beginning to be an addiction—that high, that feeling I was living two separate lives and accountable to neither. I began to see how and why men cheat, and what exactly is at stake. It's not just about sex; it's about reinventing yourself over and over again, about being new to another person, about the seductive pull of false intimacy. And, mostly, it's about believing your own lies. I knew what I was doing was wrong, but I also wanted to see how far I could take it. *I'll stop*, I told myself, *after the wedding. I just have to get it out of my system.* I told myself this over and over—as if by repeating the words, they would somehow magically become the truth. But part of me knew better. Part of me knew that I'd probably never stop cheating on him now that I'd started—it was far too late for that.

A week before the wedding date I called my father long distance. My adrenaline was pumping. I knew that my father would not be happy about what I had to say. The invitations were out, the wedding gifts were arriving at the house every day with alarming speed, the honeymoon in the Bahamas was booked, the tickets nonrefundable. I had never fully reconciled with my parents. Rather I had moved through my adolescence telling myself that I didn't need anything from them—these people I barely knew or understood. Yet here I was, practically begging for an escape hatch. I don't know why I let them pay for the wedding in the first place, why I put myself in that position of being beholden to them. I suppose I thought they owed me something.

When I heard my father's voice on the line, I burst into tears. "Dad?" I said, blowing my nose loudly into a tissue, "I don't think I can do it." There was silence on the other end of the line. "Please don't be mad at me." I could hear him whispering to my mother on his end of the line, and I closed my eyes.

"Jennifer," he said finally, taking a deep breath. "We just want you to be happy." My father and I had never been close, but at that moment, I felt he understood me. I wept loudly in gratitude and relief. The wedding was cancelled, gifts returned, dress shoved in the back of the closet where I wouldn't have to see it every day, mocking me with its virginal, unspoiled presence. To my chagrin, my resolve didn't hold out for long—I couldn't deal with the hurt in my fiancé's eyes every time I looked at him, or the constant pressure from his family to reschedule the wedding. I broke things off with my lover at the time, and took a deep breath. I rescheduled the wedding and threw myself into the preparations: flowers, cake, and honeymoon—anything so that I wouldn't have to stop and think about what I was doing. *You're getting married*, I told myself. *You have to be faithful.* And I was—but I was also totally and completely miserable.

The wedding was beautiful: acres of white roses and lilies, the cream-colored dress sparkling with discreet beading, a cathedral-length veil covering my face. As I walked down the aisle, I had the distinctly uneasy feeling I was on stage, performing a role I was woefully unprepared for. There was the honeymoon with its crystal-blue waters, the hot sand under our toes, the sounds of waves lapping gently against the shore as we slept encircled in a maze of white sheets and each other's arms. *I can do this*, I told myself watching my husband's sleeping face, touching the blond curls that fell over his forehead. *I'm a wife now.*

I returned home with the best intentions. I would look down at the ring on my finger, telling myself, *You're married now. You're someone's wife.* I told myself this when I flirted with a cute guy at a coffee house. I told myself this when he asked me for my number and when he called later that night. I repeated those words over and over again like a mantra as he fucked me later that week. They didn't help and, most importantly, they weren't enough to stop me from destroying my life.

One night I came home late—later than usual—and found my husband sitting in the kitchen in the dark, moonlight splashing over his blond features, turning his flesh silver. As I sat down beside him, I could see he was crying, silently, tears slipping down his face and landing on the Mexican-tiled floor. We sat there for a while in the dark, listening to the sounds of our breathing as our chests rose and fell in unison. I looked at the moon hanging outside the window, at the shiny set of keys still in my hand—anything to avoid looking at his face. When he finally spoke, his voice was careful and measured. "Just how many guys have you been sleeping with?" My blood ran cold and my heart literally stopped in my chest. I looked down at my hands and began furiously picking at my cuticles. I didn't answer. I didn't know what to say. Hearing the tremor in his voice I knew I'd done enough damage. Giving him names, dates, and locations wouldn't have helped us fix something that, by this point, was irreparable.

We cried in each other's arms, the tears sliding from the corners of my eyes and falling faster and faster with the knowledge that it was really over, the knowledge of what I'd lost finally smacking me in the face with a kind of clarity that made me want to curl up in a ball and wail. The pain of what I'd done was overwhelming—I didn't know how I was ever going to live with it.

We were divorced a few months later. No amount of apologizing would have been enough to save our marriage. I'd learned the hard way that the fundamental basis of a relationship rests on trust, and once that trust is violated it can rarely be repaired. So many years have passed, and what stays with me about my twenties is the incredible selfishness I displayed when it came to love, when it came to *myself*. For the first time I saw that my actions had consequences, which could—sometimes in extremely negative ways—affect others.

The day the bouquet arrived, encased behind that thick, transparent glass, I did the unthinkable: I smashed it. I don't know where the impulse came from, all I *do* know is that all of a sudden I was filled with rage and regret. That long-dead bouquet was mocking me: dead flowers, dead marriage. The softly curving gilded frame reminded me of a coffin, or a lock of a dead lover's preserved hair, forever sealed under glass, untouchable, unchanged by time or circumstance. I didn't stop to think—I picked up a book and threw it as hard as I could. The glass shattered into a thousand little shards across the beige carpet. For days, as I moved heavy boxes and furniture into a truck I had rented, I pulled pieces of glass from the bottoms of my feet, from the rubber soles of my flat shoes—so unlike the delicate, high-heeled slippers I'd worn on my wedding day.

It felt just.

BIOGRAPHIES

JENNIFER BANASH lives, works, and writes in Iowa City, Iowa, where she is a doctoral candidate in English literature at the University of Iowa. She authored the novel *Hollywoodland: An American Fairy Tale* and co-runs Impetus Press, a publishing company specializing in books that fall contentedly somewhere between the elite literature of the literati and mass-market paperbacks. Born and raised in New York City, Jennifer has also resided in Phoenix, Arizona. Jennifer—who shares her home with a beagle named Sigmund, a great listener—is happily unmarried.

JOSHUA M. BERNSTEIN, a Brooklyn-based freelance writer, says he spends his days puttering around his apartment in boxer briefs, checking email every two minutes, and eating his roommate's cold pizza. In his more adventurous moods, he publishes the zine *Rated Rookie*, gets drunk for the *New York Press*, eats himself into a coma for *Time Out New York*, cares about the environment for *Plenty*, and pens the occasional puff piece about dolls. Yes, dolls. And sometimes teddy bears. Luckily, his parents are very proud of him, and they're finally able to acknowledge that he once edited porn. In his essay, Joshua describes the deleterious effect this disreputable occupation had on him—a recent college grad, new to New York City. Writing "Non-Babe in Pornland" brought him down, pun intended, almost as much as the actual experience did.

*

NICK BURD is a fiction graduate of the MFA writing program at the New School. He lives in Brooklyn and works for the Pen American Center, the world's oldest human rights organization and the oldest international literary organization. Nick is currently at work on a novel. His worst job, however, entailed adhering stickers onto puppy calendars. Playing and touring with a band, not by any means among the most evil of his employments, did engender some tumultuous times—times he'd managed to forget until scribbling down this story. Nick can also bend his fingers back really far. This skill comes in handy at cocktail parties.

*

VINCE DARCANGELO, who hails from the suburbs of Pittsburgh, is an award-winning writer and the managing editor of an alternative newsweekly. In his essay, he describes the night he decided to quit using drugs. Vince made the slow transformation from user to addiction counselor...to writer. Though a journalist by trade, he still works for the Addiction Recovery Center, putting hours in on Saturdays and major holidays. Vince says his essay is not a moral tale, nor is it intended to be sad, tragic, or inspirational. It's more of a sitcom-type moment of self-awareness, when you look around the room and say, "I've got to get some new friends." Vince says he can't imagine having grown up in a world without professional wrestling.

●

CAITLIN DOUGHERTY is a twenty-five-year-old, ex-Peace Corps volunteer from a small town in Montana. Caitlin spent two years in Togo, Africa, followed by a traveling stint through northern Africa and Europe. She labels her childhood self "odd," teeter-tottering with worms and pecking dead fish. As an adult, she misses the carelessness of her early years, especially during her time waiting tables at TGI Fridays. She has no comment when asked about her flare. As revealed in her essay, she dreams of becoming a professional writer, but Caitlin, currently enrolled in a pre-med program, also hopes to one day work for Doctors Without Borders. She is currently seeking French conversation partners or Togo-enthusiasts.

●

MARK R. DYE, who hails from Honolulu, Hawaii, remembers unearthing a packet of meticulously drawn sci-fi characters dating from the fifties in the attic of his childhood home. The excitement of that moment of discovery has become the yardstick on which to measure happiness and success. Very few events have lived up to it. Mark is the author of the book *College and the Art of Partying*, an attempt at guilt-free gratification. It was, he says, a partially successful try. Mark works as a technical and freelance writer in Austin, Texas, where he has found himself contentedly settled.

MATTHEW FARWELL is currently serving as an infantryman with the 10th Mountain Division in Afghanistan. He shares a concrete and plywood room with "nine crazy infantrymen"—digs not too different from the dumps he lived in during college. Previously Matthew was an Echols Scholar at the University of Virginia and a Davis Scholar at the United World College of the American West; he also played competitive beer pong. Raised in Utah, Turkey, Germany, Virginia, and New Mexico, Matthew comes from a line of military men, his father and brother also having served in the Army. He enjoys long walks on the beach and deep meaningful conversation.

.●

REBECCA LANDWEHR is a Denver-based freelance writer who's spent more than ten years covering the Mile High City first as a business reporter at the *Denver Business Journal* and most recently as senior editor at *5280 Magazine*. At her worst job, an intern for a trade magazine, her hardhearted boss, also "Rebecca," forced her to go by "Reba." Rebecca's own quarter-life crisis happened at age twenty-eight when she left her childhood sweetheart and the comforting cocoon of that ten-year relationship. The good news—she survived. Rebecca is now happily married, stepmom to an amazing seven year old, and new mom to Baby Asher. She also finally paid off more than $23,000 in credit-card debt wracked up during her roaring twenties.

●

HARMON LEON is the author of *The Harmon Chronicles*, which won a 2003 Independent Publishers Award for \mor, as well as *Republican Like Me*, which also won Independent Publisher's Award for humor in 2005. ⸱mon's latest book, *The Infiltrator*, was released fall of 2006. He has also penned stories for *Esquire, Stuff, Salon,* NPR's *This American Life, Details, Maxim, High Times, Hustler, Penthouse, Black Book, Cosmopolitan,* and *Wired.* Harmon has performed comedy around the world, including the United Kingdom, Ireland, Canada, the Netherlands, and Denmark, and has appeared in solo shows at such places as the Montreal, Edinburgh, and Melbourne Comedy Festivals. He's appeared on *The Howard Stern Show,* Penn & Teller's *Bullshit, The Jamie Kennedy Experiment, Blind Date,* as well as the BBC. Harmon is low in sodium and perfect for the elderly.

●

JARED JACANG MAHER has worked as an associate editor for *Adbusters Magazine* and as a scriptwriter and assistant producer for Free Speech TV, and was a 2003 fellow at the Academy for Alternative Journalism. He has written for *Punk Planet, Clamor,* and Alternet.org, and served as coeditor of the literary anthology *Life and Limb: Skateboarders Write from the Deep End.* For the first time, Jared wrote about his family in his story for *Generation What?* He particularly enjoyed describing his father's unique laugh, which, he says, is in itself funny. Jared currently lives in Denver, Colorado, where he is a staff writer at *Westword.*

●

JUSTIN MAKI acquired a four-year bachelor's degree without learning a thing about agriculture, engineering, medicine, law, business, political science, or geography. After graduation, he inexplicably found himself in Japan, somewhat confused yet intrigued, and ended up staying for four years. While teaching English conversation in public schools, he used holidays for his first exploratory travels outside the United States. He has been lost in numerous countries. At present writing, Justin may be spotted somewhere along the Dalmatian Coast of Croatia.

Justin surprised himself when it took several drafts to finish "Salvation in Wordplay." He wonders if the way he understood the events described in it lacked either perception or honesty.

●

COURTNEY MARTIN is a writer, teacher, and filmmaker. Her book, *Perfect Girls, Starving Daughters: The Frightening Normalcy of Hating Your Body*, came out in April 2007. One of her essays appears in *We Don't Need Another Wave: Dispatches from the Next Generation of Feminists*. Her work has also turned up in *The New York Times, The Christian Science Monitor*, NPR, *The Village Voice, Publisher's Weekly, Clamor Magazine, Bust*, and *Bitch Magazine*. She is the co-director/producer of two short documentaries, *Stuck in Harlem* and *Letter to My Mother*. Courtney has a master of arts degree from the Gallatin School at New York University and a bachelor of arts degree from Barnard College. She is currently an adjunct professor of women's studies at Hunter College.

Writing "11.2.04" made Courtney realize how naïve, and then devastated, she was at that time in her life. She is currently neither naïve nor devastated. Courtney's brother surprised her by making such a central appearance in the essay. They used to write dirty words on the wall of the attic in their childhood home.

●

HAL NIEDZVIECKI is a Toronto-based writer and editor. He is the fiction editor and founding editor of *Broken Pencil*, the magazine of zine culture and the independent arts, and co-founder of the annual Canzine Festival of

Underground Culture. He is the author of six books, most recently *Hello, I'm Special: How Individuality Became the New Conformity* and the novel *The Program.* Afraid of what writing about this time in his life would dredge up, Hal has avoided it until now. At the same time, he says he's probably been writing about this era in his life ever since without realizing it.

•

CATHERINE STRAWN, who still can't drive by her family's first house that the tacky new owners have cruelly disfigured, grew up in Canton, Ohio. She earned her bachelor and master of arts degrees from the Medill School of Journalism at Northwestern University. Catherine briefly lived in South Africa, reporting on lifestyle, health, and social issues for *The Star* in Johannesburg and the *Weekend Argus* in Cape Town. She now works at *Jane Magazine* as an assistant research editor in New York City, and lives in a one-room apartment that pales in comparison to the beautiful Tudor domicile of her infancy. She says her favorite food is peanut butter.

•

KATE TORGOVNICK writes investigative features for *Jane Magazine*, and her articles have also appeared in *The New York Observer, British Glamour, The Village Voice,* and the *New York Daily News.* For the past year, Kate has traveled across the country, following three college cheerleading squads for her upcoming book, *Making the Castle.* At a low period in her life, Kate wrote and coded spam email, one of which she received herself. She got fired from that job. Kate originally hails from Durham, North Carolina, but left the South for Barnard College in New York City and has stayed there ever since. In addition to writing, Kate loves discovering new bands, swimming competitively, watching bad sci-fi films from the eighties, and playing with Rubik's Cubes.

•

BESS VANRENEN works as an assistant editor at Rowman & Littlefield Publishers. She received her master of arts degree in English literature from the University of Colorado at Boulder in 2004. She has lived in New Jersey, Egypt, Nevada, Florida, New York, and France. She had a brief stint waiting tables at a TGI Fridays in Paris, where she saw a small cockroach climbing across a tray of apple fritters. Her French coworkers seemed unperturbed. She has also worked a paper route (for one night), smiled at and greeted IHOP customers (where she received the laurels, "Employee of the Month"), chauffeured packages around her college campus and later sub sandwiches (though she was convinced the selling of sandwiches merely disguised the selling of more interesting, albeit illegal, substances), and provided elderly folks with debatably humorous holiday cards.

•

ERIKA T. WURTH is thirty years old and lives in Iowa City, commuting to her job as a creative writing professor at Western Illinois University. She is a mixed-blood Indian woman (Apache, Chickasaw, Cherokee), and was raised in a small town in Colorado, although she has lived in different places off and on. Erika has published poetry in *SAIL*, *AMCRJ*, and *Cedar Hill Review* and fiction in *Fiction*, *Raven Chronicles*, and *Pembroke*. Her book, *Indian Trains*, is soon to be published.

Erika says writing this essay provided her with a chance to reconstruct some of the stories she has woven together about herself. She knows, though, it's just one of many tales she could tell.

For a complete catalog of our books please contact us at:

speck press
po box 102004
denver, co 80250, usa
e: books@speckpress.com
t & f: 800-996-9783
w: speckpress.com

Our books are available through your local bookseller.